CW00602132

"*The State We Are In* is a *must* read for anyone who wants to understand the struggle within Islam and of the British Muslim community. It's the right book at the right time. Aftab Malik has brought together major Muslim religious and intellectual leaders who provide a frank, self-critical, and provocative analysis and commentary on major issues: from what does it mean to be British and a Muslim to militant Islam, the failures of their community and of the British government."

— **JOHN L. ESPOSITO**
Professor of Religion and International Affairs,
Professor of Islamic Studies, Founding Director of
the Prince Alwaleed bin Talal Center for Muslim-Christian
Understanding, Georgetown University

"With sound reason and strong faith, Aftab Ahmad Malik has moved the world one step closer to global peace, while fighting for the soul of Islam itself. *The State We Are In* constitutes a type of 'State of the *Umma* (Muslim community) Address' to which, fortunately, we are all privy. Malik and other contributors skillfully deconstruct the philosophy of some modern Islamic fundamentalists and extremists, using fourteen centuries of Muslim scholarship. Simultaneously, the writers convincingly present the world-wide *umma* as an ethical body upholding traditional Muslim values of balance, justice, mercy, and peace.

Shedding needed light on Islamic traditions of jihad, just war, and martyrdom, this book should be welcomed by students and scholars, politicians and theologians, Muslims and non-Muslims. All seekers of peace are implicitly urged to strive for the high ground of moral integrity, where authentic inner peace paves the way for authentic outward peace."

— **EILEEN EPPIG,** SSND, PHD
Associate Professor of Religious Studies
College of Notre Dame of Maryland

"Islam's first teaching was 'read,' a sophisticated response against ignorance and an encouragement for understanding. Understanding Islam, both by Muslims and others, has never been more needed than today. This collection of papers responds to various issues, which, if not addressed and appreciated, may lead to increased misunderstanding—within Muslims and internationally. To Muslims, the book offers an opportunity to be circumspect of the theological inconsistencies that embarrass Islam and Muslims. To all others, the book intelligently offers a flavor of what Islam does stand for."

— **ALI ADNAN IBRAHIM**
Adjunct Professor & Fulbright Scholar,
Georgetown University Law Center

"As Shaykh Hamza Yusuf humorously stated some years ago, 'Every Tom, Dick, and Abdallah is issuing fatwas today.' The most destructive aspects of this, of course, has been that of Muslim extremists who have not only called for but actually brought about death for so many. In response, many Muslims have spoken out against extremism and terrorism. Yet all too often those who have denounced extremism have not actually possessed the full mastery of the tradition to be able to convey in a convincing way how and why the 'fatwas' of the extremists violate both the letter and the spirit of the Islamic tradition.

The volume here fills that gap, and does so admirably. Our world today, Muslim and beyond, craves authenticity. The scholars gathered here have walked the fine line of tapping into the authentic teachings of Islam in countering extremism without falling into the trap of dogmatism. It is a remarkable achievement, resulting in a collection that deserves to be not only read, but also internalized by Muslims, educators, and policy makers.

The opposite of extremism is not a neutered sense of 'moderation.' It is, rather, a realization of the power of religion to be an illuminated and illuminating path, leading humanity back towards the Divine. For far too long, Muslims opposing extremism have contented themselves with saying what Islam does *not* say. Here we get a beautiful vision of what the tradition has said, and is saying, for all those who have ears to hear, eyes to see, and hearts to perceive."

— **OMID SAFI**
Assistant professor of Islamic Studies,
Colgate University, Hamilton, NY

Reviews from the First Edition

"… an unusually frank book produced from within the Muslim community … a useful answer to those who argue that Muslims are not prepared to face up to, and debate the difficult issues of our times …"

— **RICHARD BONNEY**
Professor of Modern History,
University of Leicester

"… Malik is to be congratulated on identifying a new generation of western Muslim thinkers at ease with the social sciences and mainstream Sunni scholarship. An indispensable point of entry for policy makers, academics and the general reader."

— **PHILIP LEWIS**
Honorary Visiting Lecturer, Department of Peace Studies,
Bradford University

"In our current crisis it is imperative to hear sensible Muslim voices. This short book is a collection of such voices and its contents include pertinent social and political analysis as well as theological judgments and guidance. The Muslim community, indeed British society, needs to attend to both kinds of reflection."

— **TARIQ MODOOD**
Professor of sociology, politics and public policy,
University of Bristol

"This thought-provoking collection of writings identifies and interrogates the complex reality and rhetoric of Islamic political radicalism in Britain today. Through a searching examination, it challenges the apparent monopoly on interpreting the faith that is claimed by Islamic radicals, and exposes the degree of misunderstanding that exists, among both Muslims and non-Muslims with respect to the concept of jihad […]. Importantly, it does not pull its punches as far as critiquing government policy and exposing the limitations of current British Muslim leadership are concerned. As this collection makes clear, how to be British and Muslim—and what 'being

Muslim' more generally means—are key 'life or death' questions facing Britain at the start of the twenty-first century, questions that none of us can afford to ignore, whether Muslim or not."

— **HUMAYUN ANSARI**
Professor of Islam and Cultural Diversity,
Royal Holloway, University of London

"This timely book explores the tragic and traumatic events of 7/7. It contains both a social scientific analysis and traditional exegesis of the Quran and the Sunna written by concerned Muslim scholars. These analyses are insightful for both Muslims and non-Muslims attempting to position the phenomena of British-born Muslims turning to 'terror'. The book is an impassioned plea for the reassertion of the mainstream values of traditional Islam to prevail against extremism, placing such values in the context of British multiculturalism and democracy."

— **RON GEAVES**
Professor of Religion,
Liverpool Hope University

THE STATE WE ARE IN

Beware of extremism in religion; for it was extremism in religion that destroyed those who went before you.

SAYING OF THE PROPHET MUHAMMAD ﷺ

THE STATE WE ARE IN

IDENTITY, TERROR & THE LAW OF JIHAD

Introduction
TAHIR ABBAS

Edited by
AFTAB AHMAD MALIK

First published in 2006
This updated and expanded edition published 2008

Amal Press, PO Box 688, Bristol BS99 3ZR, England

http://www.amalpress.com
info@amalpress.com

A catalogue record for this book is available from the British Library

ISBN 13: 978-0-9540544-7-2 paperback
ISBN 13: 978-0-9540544-8-9 cloth

Special thanks to Valerie J. Turner

Cover image: Ridwan Adhami. Ridzdesign.com

Layout and text: Partnersinprint.co.uk

Printed and bound in Great Britain by Biddles Ltd., King's Lynn, Norfolk

CONTENTS

NOTES ON CONTRIBUTORS

'Abdallah bin Bayyah has had a long and distinguished scholarly career. He served as a judge (*qadi*) in the Ministry of Justice in Mauritania, and later moved on to become one of the vice presidents of the first president of Mauritania. He headed the sharia section in the court of appeals, and was appointed to the position of High Authority for Religious Affairs for the republic's highest office. In the years that followed, he served as the minister of National Guidance and as the Permanent Secretary of the People's Party of Mauritania. Presently, Shaykh 'Abdallah has emerged as one of the leading authorities of *fiqh al-'aqaliyat*, the science of legal rulings that relate to Muslims living as minority communities among non-Muslims. He currently lives in Jeddah where he is a professor at King Abdul Aziz University and teaches juristic methodology, Qur'anic commentary, and Arabic.

Aftab Ahmad Malik is Visiting Fellow at the Centre for Ethnicity and Culture at the University of Birmingham. He is the editor of three books: *With God on Our Side: Politics & Theology of the War on Terrorism* (2005); *The Empire and the Crescent: Global Implications for a New American Century* (2003); and *Shattered Illusions: Analysing the War on Terrorism* (2002). He is the author of *The Broken Chain: Reflections upon the Neglect of a Tradition* (2001). Aftab has served as a consultant for various organisations on issues relating to Muslim extremism, most recently for the United Nations. His ongoing research into the rise of anti-Semitism in the modern Muslim world is being conducted at the Centre for Ethnicity and Culture. He was recently invited by the C-100 group (Council of 100 Leaders: West-Islamic Dialogue) to speak at the World Economic Forum and the Institute of Defence and Strategic Studies in Singapore.

David Dakake is an American Muslim who is a specialist in Comparative Religion and Islamic Philosophy. He has an MA in Religious

Studies from Temple University and is currently a PhD candidate in their Religious Studies Programme. He has published several articles on Islamic history and philosophy and delivered academic papers in the Middle East, Europe and North America. He currently teaches in the Religious Studies Department at George Mason University in Fairfax, Virginia.

Gibril F. Haddad is a well-known Lebanese–American scholar and religious leader. Schooled in England, he took his PhD degree from Columbia University in New York, before embarking on an intensive study of hadith, Islamic law and doctrine under leading authorities of the Middle East.

H.A. Hellyer is Senior Research Fellow of the Centre for Research in Ethnic Relations at the University of Warwick (UK). He was Visiting Professor of Law at the American University in Cairo (Egypt) and Ford Fellow at the Brookings Institution in Washington, DC (USA). A prolific commentator and researcher of classical Islamic law, Dr. Hellyer is the author of the forthcoming "The 'Other' European: Multiculturalism and Muslims" to be published by Edinburgh University Press.

Hamza Yusuf is considered as one of the foremost contemporary spokespersons for Islam. He has translated into English several classical Arabic texts. In addition, he has served as the principal lecturer at religious intensive seminars in America, England, Spain, and Morocco. Shaykh Hamza also founded The Zaytuna Institute and Academy which has established an international reputation for presenting a classical picture of Islam in the West and which is dedicated to the revival of traditional study methods and the sciences of Islam.

Muhammad Afifi al-Akiti was born in Malaysia and was educated from a young age in the classical Islamic sciences at scholastic madrasas of East Java with a long tradition in Shafi'i jurisprudence. Among the best known authorities with whom he studied were the jurists, theologians and Sufis: Imam al-Fadani, Shaykh Ibn Mahfuz al-Hajini, and Habib 'Aydarus al-Habshi. He has travelled widely; and in addition to the specific licenses to teach (*ijazas*) from his systematic training, he has also received general licenses from teachers beyond his homeland, especially in Morocco and the Middle East. Shaykh Afifi is presently a Research Fellow in Islamic Theology at the Oxford Centre for Islamic Studies and teaches at Oxford University. His doctoral thesis investigates a newly discovered medieval manuscript of an advanced theological work by Islam's greatest theologian, Imam al-Ghazali.

Suheil Laher was born and raised in Zimbabwe in a family of Indian descent, and has lived in America for the past 15 years. He works as a software engineer, and since 1997 has served as Muslim Chaplain at the Massachusetts Institute of Technology in Cambridge, Massachusetts. His continual study of Islam has taken him to both traditional and academic settings. He has received several licenses to teach (*ijazas*), and is currently a graduate student in Religious Studies at Boston University.

Tahir Abbas is Reader (2006-) in Sociology and the founding Director of the Centre for the Study of Ethnicity and Culture (2003-) at the University of Birmingham. He has published four authored and (co-) edited books, and over eighty articles, chapters or book reviews in sociology, education, public policy and Islamic Studies. In 2006, he was sent to Indonesia and Singapore and in 2007, to Pakistan, as part of a British Muslim Delegation sponsored by the Foreign and Commonwealth Office and the British Council to help improve understanding between Britain and the Muslim world. He is a regular contributor to the media and policy debates, and was elected to the Royal Society of Arts in 2006. In 2007, he was elected to the Muslim Power 100; a list of leading Muslim lights in Britain today. His most recent publications include *The Education of British South Asians* (2004); and as editor, *Islamic Political Radicalism* (2007) and *Muslim Britain* (2005); and as co-editor, *Immigration and Race Relations: Sociological Theory and John Rex* (2007). His forthcoming book, *British Islam*, explores how the policies and practices of multiculturalism and failed foreign policies have negatively impacted on Muslim minority experiences.

Yahya Birt is currently the Director of the City Circle, a London-based network for Muslim professionals, that runs cultural, educational and welfare projects, is a part-time Research Fellow at the Islam in Europe Unit at the Islamic Foundation, Markfield, Leicestershire, UK and a member of *Islamica* Magazine's Editorial Board. He has written for the *Sunday Times, Prospect* magazine, the *New Statesman*, the *Spectator*, openDemocracy, *Q-News, Muslim News*, and alt.muslim. He has written in several academic collections and journals on various aspects of British Islam. He maintains a blog, Musings on the Britannic Crescent, and an archive of his writings at www.yahyabirt.com.

INTRODUCTION TO THE SECOND EDITION

Islamic Political Radicalisation in Britain: Appraising an Emergent Phenomenon

TAHIR ABBAS

AT A TIME of ever-rapid globalisation, identity questions for Muslim minorities in Western European nation-states, and in particular in Britain since the events of 7/7 are at the forefront of debates in policy, government, media, civil society and academia. Debates have emerged on radicalisation, secularisation, modernisation, identity conflicts, inter-generational change, cultural relativism, and social and economic exclusion.[1] Islamic political radicalism is a phenomenon of particular interest in various governmental departments, political and societal organisations and communities. There is considerable concern that this problem, however one might define it, is especially acute and a cause for alarm. Those at the left of the political spectrum believe that the "war on terror" and structural inequalities are at the heart of the problem while those on the right feel that it is the essence of Islam that is regarded as alien, barbaric, or ill-adjusted to the expectations and aspirations of the West. There is a considerable grey area in between. The fact is that Islam has very little to do with this radicalisation. Rather the issue is more about political disenfranchisement, limited material opportunities for isolated British Muslims, psychological issues, and indeed, foreign policy.[2]

It has been over two years since the events of 7/7 and the picture that is now emerging is clearer than ever. Initially, emphasis was placed on

[1] Tahir Abbas, ed., *Muslim Britain: Communities under Pressure* (London and New York: Zed, 2005).

[2] Tahir Abbas, ed., *Islamic Political Radicalism: A European Perspective* (Edinburgh: Edinburgh University Press, 2007).

Muslim identity issues, the role of mosques and leadership. Now, greater empirical research and conjectural evidence suggests that these identity issues affect non-Muslim minorities in similar ways; confidence and trust in the nation-state that brings about effective engagement and participation is a key missing element. The role of mosques is important, not in how they have apparently radicalised young people but because they have systematically failed to recognise young Muslims *per se*, and thus these issues are more about professionalisation and capacity-building. The concerns in relation to leadership are ongoing, but one must remember that leaders do not emerge out of the ether; often they become members of the elite before engaging in the political, cultural, or intellectual worlds, and with many Muslims trapped in conditions of social and economic deprivation, producing true leaders is a slow process. In addition, one needs to remain aware of the role of false leaders or puppets that were created as part of the colonial experience in Muslim lands; some of that still exists today in the post-colonial experience of Muslim minorities in Western European nation-states.

While the burgeoning analytical, empirical, and conceptual developments to theory, policy, and practice continues, Muslims are looking *within* the British Muslim community to determine what might be at fault, at the same time examining the foreign policies of the Western nation-states that have created havoc in Muslim lands. The global theatre has played out the self-fulfilling prophecy of the "clash of civilisations" thesis originally formulated by neo-conservative ideologues, such as Bernard Lewis, Samuel Huntington and Francis Fukyuyama. The stark realities of the 1990s and the early years of the twenty-first century have revealed the immeasurable suffering of Muslims around the world. From the first Gulf War (1990–1991) to Somalia (1993), Bosnia-Herzegovina (1993–1996), Chechnya (1999), the second Palestinian Intifada (2000–), the war on Afghanistan (2001–2002) and the war on Iraq (2003–), Muslims have been on the receiving end of the political and economic interests of Western hegemony. Twenty million Muslims in Western Europe and six million in the United States have witnessed various reactions to this onslaught—some internally-derived others externally influenced.

From attacks on the Paris metro (1996), to the Moscow theatre attack (2002), the Madrid bombings (2004) that killed 192 people, and the assassination of Theo van Gogh (2004), we then had the first ever suicide-bombings by home-grown radicals in London in 2005. Some have argued that this is "Blair's blowback". This was not the first time British-born Muslim political radicals have come to the fore; the Yemen Seven (1999) included five British-born Muslims, the two failed shoe bombers Richard Reid and Saajid Badat, and the 2003 "Mike's Place" bombers in Tel Aviv from Derby and Hounslow (Omar Khan Sharif and Asif Mohammed Hanif).

We can identify earlier periods of this so-called radicalisation of Islam, particularly in the twentieth century, in the writings of Muslim ideologues of the 1940s or 1950s, or the actions of the Palestinian Liberation Organisation and its wings of the Popular Front for the Liberation of Palestine and Fateh in the 1960s and 1970s, or in the activities of the Libyans, Iraqis, Iranians or the Lebanese (through Hamas or Hezbollah) in the 1980s. There is a perceptible pattern in which Muslims in Islamic lands have reacted against the oppression of invading forces, the double standards of outside democratic regimes, and the dominant interests of powerful capitalistic nations vying for control over the remaining natural fossil fuels of the world. For the last three decades, from the Iranian Revolution of 1979 onwards, the Muslim world has been in turmoil while Muslim minorities in the West have been economically, socially, politically and culturally marginalised. It is these harsh experiences that characterise our sociological, anthropological, cultural and political interests in the study of Muslims, especially in Britain today.

The London terror outrage now known as 7/7 made it apparent that the threat from suicide bombers comes not only from foreigners who supposedly slip into the country under the radar of security and surveillance, but from people who have grown up and live amongst us. These are fellow citizens, willing to die so they can kill others. How and why British-born Muslims, of whatever ethnicity, class or cultural hue, would want to do this is difficult to understand, though understand it we must if we are to prevent these acts in the future. There are a number of factors which we can recognise, not just from the London bombings but from others elsewhere. It is a complex jigsaw puzzle, but we can at least place some of the pieces together.

First, there is the psychological and emotional brainwashing of individuals through the radicalising messages of those claiming Islamic knowledge.

This brainwashing encourages the killing of innocent people for infinite rewards in paradise or as part of an act of war. The Jihadi-Salafi types, those whose literal interpretation of Islam is locked-tight, are the essential drivers in this radicalisation of Muslims, in both the West and elsewhere. Muslims, whether as minorities or majorities in countries throughout the world, feel a perceptible strain, because sharia law is frozen and Islam is closed off to the rest of humanity. It was not always like this, of course, but one would have to look back nine hundred years to Muslim Spain to find an open and inclusive Islam. The Islam that is practised today has been impoverished by five hundred years of imperialism and colonialism. We live in the "dark ages" of Islam and the methods used by fundamentalists, Islamists or radicals to seek redress are abysmally outmoded in a world that has moved on. It is important to emphasise nevertheless, that the actions of these terrorists are almost entirely political and not at all theological. These Muslims are driven to do what they do because they believe they will go to heaven, and in the process create political change by encouraging the world's leaders to take action on Iraq specifically, but also in Palestine, Chechnya and Kashmir; all as part of the wider struggle to liberate Muslims from the daily oppression they currently experience.

Second, given the predicaments of exclusion, it is nevertheless apparent that there is a genuine failure of leadership at home, in the community, and at the local and national levels. Leadership in the Muslim population is determined by the pandering of British politicians to elites who are often of a very different make-up and outlook than the many they seek to represent. Local community "elders" are propped up through artificial support mechanisms that facilitate the electoral process to the advantage of the main political parties but remove free choice from the hands of the people. Religious leadership has also been weak. The imams in mainstream mosques are not central, if relevant at all, to the leadership of Muslims, and are certainly not responsible for the radicalising of the young. They are most poorly-equipped to fulfil their role in the religious, cultural and intellectual edification of young people. This failing makes young people vulnerable to Islamists who have been able to fill the gap. The opportunity for imams to be the educators of the community, in the Qur'ānic texts and as Muslims living in the West, has been missed and Muslim communities are poorer for it.

Third, the role of the media is important. It is perfectly possible for an individual to grow up in an insulated environment, where the television, Internet, food, community and local enterprise are entirely Muslim. A young man can be radicalised by images of victims in Palestine or Chechnya from the comfort of his own home, through conversations within a circle of friends with similar perspectives on life or by reading the many pieces of imbalanced literature that are freely available. This is one of the consequences of globalisation: we are connected to every aspect of this planet through communication technology, but we have lost touch with our neighbours in the process. Where the media encloses Muslims at one level, at another it spreads Islamophobia—not least by focusing on preachers from the wilder fringes of Islam rather than the more recognised authorities. Few commentators are able to distinguish between the Islam that is practiced in general and the disturbed Islam that is practiced by the very few, yet these commentators remain the prominent critics of the religion. This conceals the fact that there is wide-ranging debate within Islam about modernity. The Western critique, relentless as it is ill-informed, hinders rather than facilitates this debate.

Fourth, at the national and international levels, the problem has been exacerbated by the "war on terror" launched after the 9/11 attacks on America. The coalition of the willing has taken it upon itself, with little or no support from the rest of the world, to weed out "Islamic" terror, bringing freedom (of markets) and democracy (of sorts) to ailing nations. Attacks first on Afghanistan and then on Iraq have made Muslims feel that they are soft targets, part of an unadulterated US-led assault. Late modernity's cultural, economic and political hegemon needs a bogey to legitimise its laissez-faire machinations and after the end of the cold war Islam is that bogey. In the aftermath of 9/11, with increased policing powers, advanced electronic surveillance techniques, the elimination of habeas corpus and challenges to Muslim loyalty to the state, Muslims in Western nation-states have become victims of the aggressive state apparatus.

Muslims in the West are in a precarious position because of the combination of these internal and external dynamics, the juxtaposition of the local, national and international. They see the wider Islamic world in tatters and their own experiences affected by dominant negative domestic paradigms, but in reality "mainstream" Islam has no answers. What a few young Muslim people, mostly men, do is seek solutions to their frustrations in violence and destruction. Little do they realise that they help no one and only create further distress, disharmony and disillusionment. It is quite apparent that Islam in the West, and elsewhere, is in need of a new impetus. Given the anti-discrimination laws of this country and the general openness of British society, one must hope that it will remain a real possibility here. Certainly, the 7/7 attacks on London have added to direct and indirect forms of Islamophobia. There is considerable evidence of violence towards individuals, communities and mosques; there has been an impact on Muslims living in Britain, particularly those who are visible adherents of marginalised communities across the country, and this has further increased fear and distrust of the majority society. But it should also act as a demonstration to the groups who would execute terrorist acts in Britain, that however hard they try they will never succeed in disrupting Britain's relatively fair, just and tolerant society and that all they have done is further vilify the name of Islam. The British multiculturalism project is still under development, but further attacks or attempted efforts by Muslims will weaken any positive gains made over the last three decades.

Indeed, as a result of the 7/7 terror attacks in London, and the failed attacks almost two years later, once again in London and in Glasgow, there has been a genuine attempt on the part of the nation-state to try and engage with its British Muslim minority, particularly the young and disaffected. Reverberations from the complete shock of the events are still being felt as communities, neighbourhoods, politicians and the state come to terms with the enormity of the events and the potential implications they have for public and social policy. What increases this distress is the discovery that the acts were orchestrated by British-born Muslims, many of whom were seemingly well-integrated citizens. This had completely bamboozled the intelligence services, who were of the view that any would-be terrorist attacks would be organised by overseas groups infiltrating networks in Britain. That these young British men were without doubt self-radicalised has come as a genuine surprise to many and, as such, makes it even more pertinent to better understand the mechanisms and processes that drove them to their actions and, more importantly for the future, to determine how best to engage with alienated British Muslims, some of whom are prepared to carry out such atrocities in the name of religion and politics. The need to understand and appreciate the depth of the dissatisfaction felt by young Muslims in Britain is more important than ever. In whatever way, Muslims and non-Muslims must move forward from here: we all need to remain aware that these bombers and the increasing number who have been prosecuted or will be in court throughout the early part of 2008 facing criminal prosecutions are indeed "made in Britain".

A chief concern with young people and the question of Islamic political radicalism is how it comes about in the first instance and then, how it can be alleviated. This is something that the nation-state seems to be making a genuine effort to understand. Perhaps it is too early to be sure of any particular steps to be taken, but the view from the communities and the professionals is that positive strides are being made. However it is also palpably clear that the questions of what drives radicalisation and how to engage with radicalised young people remain as difficult as ever to answer. The communities from which many radicals emanate are those that are generally removed from any engagement in the political process. Where there is suspicion of activity it tends to centre on the movements of shadowy figures who venture into homes late at night, presumably radicalising others. This is certainly possible given media developments in the Islamic world and the way in which the bleak truths of war can stir the imagination of young minds already susceptible to feelings of frustration, anger, hate, and ultimately capable of the will to carry out violence in its name.

In other instances, there is a perceptible view that higher education institutions are "hotbeds" of radical political Islamic activity, sometimes acting as launch pads to further radicalise young Muslims who are perhaps away from home for the first time, still somewhat naive but very much emotionally affected by the injustices of the world. Nonetheless, the question as to whether the Islamic societies of universities are actually places where Muslims are radicalised is not yet clear. Hizb ut-Tahrir (the Liberation Party) was banned from university campuses by the National Union of Students in the mid-1990s. Currently, there has been talk of banning it altogether, though the jury is still out as to whether this organisation openly propagates violent extremism. Certainly, Hizb ut-Tahrir is banned from many European countries. Today, it may well be carrying out its work covertly, infiltrating other university associations, namely Pakistani or Indian societies. But their success, overt or covert, is difficult to gauge in real terms. No suicide bombing has been carried out by any British member of Hizb ut-Tahrir, although Asif Mohammed Hanif who blew himself up in Tel Aviv in 2003 and his partner in crime, the would-be bomber, Omar Khan Sharif, were both British-born and had some links with al-Muhajiroun (a splinter group, founded in the United Kingdom in 1996 by Omar Bakri Muhammad, who now lives in voluntary exile in Syria). Many of the "Yemen Seven", who allegedly tried to blow up the British Embassy and a nightclub in Sana in 1999, were British-born Muslims. They met at university and were radicalised by Abu Hamza, formerly of Finsbury Park Mosque; he is currently awaiting deportation to the United States on terrorism related charges and is serving time in Belmarsh. Clearly, when young Muslims go away to university, it is apparent that a few do emerge very different from when they entered. The danger is in the small percentage of these people who emerge as outwardly well-integrated folk, who live and work among majority society, unbeknownst to us that they may well be potential threats to everyone, until, of course, it is far too late.

The important point is to ensure that nothing quite like the events of 7/7 ever happens again, as the repercussions would seriously reduce civil liberties, lead to ever more draconian anti-terrorist legislation and further alienate a body of young men who are already at the margins of society. To achieve success one needs to remove the barriers that prevent dialogue with young Muslim men. This conversation needs to be direct and specific; the problem is that the conduit of existing community leaders has proven to be woefully ineffective. If anything, the events of 7/7 spelt the death of the existing Muslim community leader, whether political, cultural or intellectual. The voices of Professor Tariq Ramadan and Shaykh Hamza Yusuf have been popular with both the young and the British state, but they are a small band of forward-looking Islamic scholars and their permanence in influencing the government as well as maintaining the support of the young remains a fine balance between how the nation will use these opportunities and how they are perceived by the many.

In reality, a mass of young Muslim people are dislocated and disenfranchised; this is a result of the workings of society, but more discernibly it relates to the specific ways in which they have been failed by both Muslim and non-Muslim institutions. It is perhaps pertinent that the state has realised this and has attempted to engage them in a full-on campaign of ministerial visits to Muslim-concentrated localities in the hope that it will encourage this oft-missed exchange of ideas. It now also employs Muslims in principal civil service posts in an attempt to better connect with the Muslim public at large. The nation-state has recognised that it did not have the trust of Muslims, or non-Muslims, given how most of the British population negatively views the war on Iraq (Britain has all but withdrawn its troops now, but sent more to Afghanistan). These are confidence-building, trust-enhancing, face-saving exercises for the cynics, an opportunity to better engage with a marginalised community for the pragmatists, and a desire to make a just, fair and tolerant society for the good of the many for the optimists.

In the end, the potential for Islamic political terrorism will not go away easily because the root causes are so deep-seated. They are as much a matter of economic and social concern as they are of Britain's ailing foreign policy. Under the premiership of Gordon Brown, who is less reliant on spin and genuinely has more political substance, there are positive signs. However, there is an entrenched malaise that is at the heart of many of problems of Islamic political radicalism in Europe—interventions in Muslim lands, where economic imperatives are disguised as political developments to democracy and freedom being the main. Botched Bush-Blair endeavours between 2001 and 2007 were seen as "humanitarian interventions", "necessary evils", or at the very worst, "mistakes". To have suggested anything more critical is to be considered absurd by the intelligentsia or the popular press, or even disloyal to the state. At the local level, as poorer Muslim communities are increasingly segregated, calls for the "death of multiculturalism" and a reversion to assimilationism are now increasingly heeded. Communication with young people is doomed to fail in eliminating radicalism if what is manifestly obvious in its cause is not perceptibly eliminated. The failure to act is the failure of conversation. It is also a failure to be genuinely honest about the nature of the problems and their foundations.

Politicians will be looking for initiatives in response to 7/7. Policy must seek to achieve five things: ensure that Muslim communities become more culturally and politically included than they have been; provide genuine educational and labour market opportunities for the young; make certain that community leadership is reflective and capable; certify the religious instructors in mainstream mosques, ensuring that they are properly connected with local and national institutions; and last but not least, help ensure that issues at the international level that impact British South Asian Muslims, namely Iraq, Palestine, and Kashmir, are resolved, and that peace and hope reach the affected regions. We must all work hard, Muslims and non-Muslims alike, to ensure that young Muslim men are not cut off from society and therefore do not become susceptible to fanatical, extremist and utterly misinformed Islamists that seek to politically radicalise the meek and vulnerable. One specific response has been to talk with young Muslims, particularly by generating a new class of leaders, but connecting with disaffected Muslims will not be as straightforward as it might appear.

The chapters in this book are written by renowned and evolving Muslim scholars in the field of Islamic, political and social studies. They discuss Muslims as minorities in the state in the current period, from a range of theological and sociological perspectives. These analysts are jurists, ethicists and historians who come from all over the world to address the crucial contemporary issues and challenges facing Muslims in the West with insights that draw upon the intellectual framework of a classical Islamic discourse as well the social and cultural observations they make of the world in which we all live. As such, this book is a unique collection of contributions from Muslims who have studied and worked in British, European and American universities. It is an important and useful introduction to students, academics, policymakers, commentators and political figures alike.

Part 1 THE STATE WE ARE IN

1 Islamic Citizenship in Britain after 7/7: Tackling Extremism and Preserving Freedoms

YAHYA BIRT

THE WEEKS AFTER the London bombings of 7/7, the most deadly to strike the capital since the Second World War, have been testing times for British Muslims. We struggle under a threefold burden. Like others, we nervously rang family and friends to find out if they were all right. The mangled and twisted frame of the familiar double-decker bus and the unseen horror in the Tube tunnels below London's streets signalled a new and bloody era. We learnt with shock that our own community had produced Britain's first home-grown suicide bombers, seemingly integrated British lads. Our feelings of moral outrage were tempered by profound disquiet that this had been carried out in the name of our religion. Finally, we have felt the consequences, the most fearsome part of which has not been the six hundred percent rise in faith-hate crimes in London during the first four weeks,[1] but a lurch towards draconian legislation amid talk across the political spectrum of the failure of British multiculturalism from across the political spectrum.[2]

Number 10 launched a tough strategy on 5 August 2005 which mirrors steps pioneered by the French in the mid-1990s, the Americans after 9/11 and the Spanish after the Madrid bombings. The proposed measures

[1] *Independent*, 4 August 2005. The survey of different police forces showed the rise in reported faith-hate and race-hate incidents was spread across the country, not just concentrated in the capital. As many as one in six were not Muslim by religion, but were of an Asian appearance. The number of race-hate attacks increased by 24 percent overall from 3355 in July 2004 to 4160 in July 2005.

[2] Kenan Malik, "Multiculturalism has fanned the flames of Islamic extremism", *Times*, 16 July 2005 and David Davies, "Why cultural tolerance cuts both ways", *Daily Telegraph*, 3 August 2005.

include establishing new powers to deport foreign nationals on the grounds of fomenting terrorism and involvement with proscribed extremist bookshops, organisations, websites and networks; closing extremist mosques; widening the grounds to ban extremist groups; banning Hizb ut-Tahrir and al-Muhajiroun's successor groups; stripping citizenship from naturalized British citizens engaged in extremism; creating a new offence of glorifying terrorism in Britain and abroad; and the extension of existing control orders to include British nationals, using a form of house arrest, to include British nationals. The new deportation powers would require derogation from the Article 3 of the European Convention on Human Rights prohibiting torture and inhumane treatment, in order to the guarantee the rights of deportees in some ten Muslim countries of origin, which have so far not agreed to uphold them, with the exception of Jordan.[3]

The police presence permeates an enervated London, the merits and demerits of racial profiling are openly discussed, and the shoot-to-kill policy is based on Sri-Lankan and Israeli tactics. The Home Office Minister, Hazel Blears, caught in the midst of local consultations with Muslims, is suddenly to head a commission to examine "insufficiently integrated" communities, suggesting the re-branding of minorities along ethnic lines in the style of the American melting pot.[4] Plans are mooted to charge extremist Muslim preachers under the Treason Act of 1351, the first time it would have been applied since the Second World War.

The London attacks and their aftermath are the greatest challenge to face British Muslims—the precise challenge being to reject charges of collective guilt *while* taking take up our share of responsibility. There has been much heartfelt condemnation of the attacks, as might have been expected from Muslim community and religious leaders.[5] But it is obvious to all that our older generation of leaders is out of touch with the febrile and confused sentiment apparent among many young Muslims after 7/7. Anger, denial and fantastic conspiracy theories are rife, but community

[3] Opening Statement, Prime Minister's Press Conference, 5 August 2005, No. 10 Downing Street, available at www.number-10.gov.uk/output/Page8041.asp.

[4] *Times*, 8 August 2005.

[5] A press statement condemning terrorism was issued jointly by religious scholars associated with the Muslim Council of Britain and the British Muslim Forum on 15 July, representing the largest Islamic groups in Britain, available at http://www.mcb.org.uk/Signed_Ulama_statement.pdf.

elders rarely know how to direct these sentiments in constructive directions. As for their religious responsibilities, British Muslims should seek to tackle extremism, to uphold and assist in the promotion of public safety while protecting the freedoms of all British citizens, to exonerate those who are falsely accused or unfairly treated, and to improve community relations.[6] These teachings imply a delicate balancing act that promotes a precautious but constructive engagement with the security agenda founded on the belief that preserving freedoms in a time of crisis will do more to ensure our security than hasty new measures; freedom and security need not be instinctively placed in mutual opposition with each other as Shami Chakrabarti of Liberty has argued.[7]

One matter is absolutely clear among young Muslims in the impassioned debate after 7/7: they will not accept the silencing of their political voice through a spurious culpability by association. The invasion and occupation of Iraq, as they see it, lies precisely at the centre of their current disaffection. If it is indeed true to say that global jihadist puritanism was the unwanted progeny of the Cold War's last great conflict-by-proxy in Afghanistan against the Soviets,[8] Iraq has nonetheless also opened up a whole new front in the "war on terror" that did not previously exist, as was argued in a recent report by the establishment think tank, the Royal Institute of International Affairs.[9] It is particularly relevant in that the continuing "war on terror" has invalidated the "covenant of security" the extremist fringe believed they enjoyed in Britain, which underpinned the logic of Londonistan's very existence.[10]

[6] This balanced approach of protecting both societal and community interests is upheld in a recent legal ruling from the Ḥanafī school of jurisprudence, the school of law followed by the majority of British Muslims. See Shaykh Faraz Rabbani's reply to this following question after having consulted with leading Ḥanafī authorities, "If someone knows about potential extremist plotting against public interest in a Western country, what is our duty? Would it be 'giving up on a Muslim's rights' to inform the police?", 21 July 2005, available at: http://forums.muslimvillage.net/lofiversion/index.php/t13883.html and elsewhere.

[7] Shami Chakrabarti, "The price of a chilling and counterproductive recipe", *Guardian*, 8 August 2005.

[8] For the definitive political long view see John Cooley, *Unholy Wars: Afghanistan, America and International Terrorism*, 3rd edn, with an introduction by Edward W. Said (London: Pluto, 2002).

[9] *Daily Telegraph*, 18 July 2005.

[10] For further details on the covenant of security and its so-called annulment, see the refutation of a position statement from the British Muslim group, al-Muhajiroun, by Shaykh M. Afifi al-Akiti in this collection.

Thus, the Prime Minister, vulnerable over Iraq, has found it increasingly difficult to deny that Iraq has been an aggravating political factor. However, the point is that after the attacks, while two-thirds of the British public saw Iraq as heightening the risk of terrorism in the UK, the Prime Minister received his second-highest personal approval rating since 1997.[11] This indicates that the British public saw the threats of Saddam Hussein and of radical terrorism, falsely justified in the name of Islam, as separate, and secondly, that Blair was broadly trusted to take on the post-7/7 threat, unlike the Spanish who promptly voted José Maria Aznar out of office after the Madrid bombings. Besides personal conviction on these matters, two political factors have emboldened the Prime Minister to pursue a tougher stand and take on the liberal legal establishment, human rights activists, a more precautious Home Office, and pretty much the entirety of the British Muslim community's leadership. Firstly, Blair was encouraged by the robust stance of the four-man delegation of Labour Muslim MPs led by Shahid Malik on 13 July 2005, even if they differed in terms of strategy and analysis.[12] Secondly, the wide public trust in Blair's capability to defend Britain against this threat has allowed Number 10 to set the security agenda in its own terms, advised by the former Home Secretary, David Blunkett, whose tough approach has always been endorsed by the Prime Minister. It is in this shift of public opinion that the "rules of the game" have changed.

Furthermore, unfashionable as it might be to make the observation, Tony Blair was right to argue that the London suicide bombings have no *moral* connection with Iraq. The immediate challenge for Muslims is to isolate extremist elements by returning to the ethical and moral foundations of Islam, and to argue calmly for peaceful democratic means of protest. Already in places like London and Birmingham, there are hopeful signs that a younger generation of opinion-formers like Salma Yaqoob of the Respect Party or Abu Muntasir of JIMAS (Jam'iat Ihyaa' Minhaaj al-Sunnah) are reaching out effectively by offering viable alternatives to those who feel radically disaffected by offering viable alternatives.

[11] Populus/Times Poll in *Times*, 26 July 2005.

[12] *Observer*, 7 August 2005, although there was no unanimity on all of the announced measures among the four MPs. For instance, Shahid Malik and Sadiq Khan opposed the banning of Hizb ut-Tahrir, while Khalid Mahmood supported the ban.

A full debate will be needed on the suspect theology that spreads intolerance and hatred; the input of religious leaders will be vital to this process. Another vital critical component in this regard will be to tackle the rise of *takfirism*, the rationale behind the rise of violent cults that see all other Muslims as expendable apostates. In this regard, British Muslims could look to build upon the Amman initiative of July 2005 that recognises eight orthodox schools of Islamic law; this initiative and was endorsed by major Sunni and Shiite scholars of the Arab world.[13] There are already encouraging signs that Islamic scholars and younger community leaders are disregarding old sectarian boundaries to make common cause against extremism. The old guard amongst whom petty rivalry and sectarianism remain predominant has not yet embraced this new entente.

Another key issue is the need to reclaim the high standards of ethical conduct in the jihad tradition, which, while upholding the right to self-defence, protects the innocent and condemns terrorist tactics.[14] How is it that suicide bombing, first used and justified in the Muslim world by Hezbollah in 1983, inspired by the example of the Marxist Tamil Tigers of Sri Lanka, has become the preferred tactic of resistance in the name of Islam—used in no less than twenty-six countries around the world, with Britain, unfortunately, being only the latest example?[15] Is the Muslim world in danger of becoming the West's Gaza Strip, and the West, the Muslim world's Israel, by which the nameless and unnumbered casualties of American airpower are re-invoked by desperate acts of revenge, spreading Middle Eastern-style fear and insecurity to the Western metropolis?

In holding the balance between freedom and security, as British citizens, not just as British Muslims, it is our public duty to ask some constructive

[13] International Islamic Conference (Amman), "True Islam and its Role in Modern Society", 4–6 July 2005, final conference statement, available in English translation at http://www.jordanembassyus.org/new/pr/pr07062005.shtml.

[14] For a clear differentiation between terrorism and jihad in Islamic jurisprudence, please refer to the second section of this anthology.

[15] For the full list of countries in which suicidal terrorism has taken place in the name of Islam see the 2005 report by the British Muslim think tank, Ihsanic Intelligence, *The Hijacked Caravan: Refuting Suicide Bombings as Martyrdom Operations in Contemporary Jihad Strategy*, (2005), pp. 20–21, nn. 14–15, available online at www.ihsanic-intelligence.com. The study also notes that the tactic was virtually non-existent in Sunni movements in the 1980s, but became more widespread in the early 1990s following the Palestinian lead, and has mushroomed after 9/11. Pre-9/11 suicide bombing incidents totalled 78, but there were 232 after 9/11.

but searching questions about the new agenda. We should ask: can the treatment of deportees really be guaranteed when, as the government has failed many times after 9/11 to get the agreement of Muslim nations? Is it not short-termist to merely export the problem of terrorism? Why is it deemed an unfortunate but unavoidable consequence of the new shoot-to-kill policy that further innocent lives may be lost, even after the death of a Brazilian electrician, tragically mistaken for a suicide bomber? Does not the closing of a place of worship potentially stigmatise the whole congregation as extremist, rather than dealing with a problematic preacher? With the proposal to extend control orders to British suspect extremists, do we not have a new form of internment, a policy that in Northern Ireland bolstered support for the IRA?

Particular concerns centre around free speech. In the post-7/7 atmosphere, how would any "incitement to religious hatred" legislation be applied? Or for that matter "glorifying terrorist acts"? Would this, for instance, cover any number of examples involving struggles for self-determination in the Muslim world? What might be the consequences for Britain's grand tradition of political asylum if new proscribed speech-acts or activities result in rapid deportation? How will the process of proscription of designated extremist bookshops, websites, centres and networks be held up to proper scrutiny? Can we name any non-violent political organisation that has been banned since the Second World War despite the challenges of the Cold War and Irish Republicanism? If not, why is Hizb ut-Tahrir being singled out now?

The proposal to ban Hizb ut-Tahrir would, if enacted alongside these other measures, drive radicalism further underground, and in a more subtle way, muzzle Muslim political protest through fearful self-censorship. If Hizb ut-Tahrir is not considered by Scotland Yard sources to be part of the terrorist problem, the conclusion is that the ban is political. Inevitable comparisons are being made with the British National Party. British Muslims might therefore conclude that their politics was being criminalized too, and associated by the official mind with terrorism. The ban tells us something else that is disturbing: that unlike the cohesive movement of Irish Republicanism, in which the political wing had a moderating impact on the IRA, the government's judgement is that extremist, radical and moderate currents among British Muslims are too disaggregated from each other to justify a strategy of encapsulation. In other words, the government believes that while Hizb ut-Tahrir contributes to a general atmosphere of radicalisation, it cannot recall the extremists from violence anymore than the moderates can. Thus the onus is upon the party to admit to its confrontational and radicalising role prior to 1996 (when Omar Bakri Muhammad left to found al-Muhajiroun) and to become committed to a preventative strategy in future.

The symbolic weight of Hizb ut-Tahrir's banning for the Muslim community would probably vitiate the opportunity to promote an intelligence-led approach and thereby squander the widespread goodwill among Muslim communities in the wake of the bombings. What would be left except for heavy policing and therefore further alienation? The effective exclusion thus far of British Muslims from the new security agenda reveals how much the very community most likely to be impacted by these policies is held in distrust and suspicion.

In the British context, however, the condemnation of terrorism, and indeed the constructive criticism of anti-terrorism measures, should not be allowed to halt the serious working-through of issues around of identity, belonging and citizenship by cosmopolitan Muslim Britons aware too of their religious solidarity. The question is being asked: can solidarity to the *umma* be affirmed as part of British Muslim identity, as a matter of civic conscience rather than of cosmic or geopolitical alterity? It would be fruitless to place loyalties to umma and nation in political opposition, and therefore to portray this purported dichotomy as an ever-present existential crisis of cultural identity for British Muslims. At a time when national sentiment is eroded by commodification, devolution, relations with Europe, cultural diversity, globalisation, even by a collective failure of the imagination, is it just or fair to expect minority groups to bear disproportionately the burdens of nationhood in moments of crisis like this?

It is precisely this expectation that currently shapes the debate around the integration (often nowadays a euphemism for assimilation) of British Muslims, and it constitutes a political bear-trap. After 7/7, as after 9/11, the problems of our various communities are held to be our own, and these are problems of cultural backwardness. The tropes of nineteenth-century anti-Semitism re-emerge in the form of twenty-first century Islamophobia: they mistreat their women, they illiberally uphold harsh rites and a merciless law, their loyalties are suspect and lie beyond those of the nation-state.[16] These assumptions threaten to overtake official discourse about Muslim integration: Muslims are silenced in this debate; they are more talked about and dissected by others in an endless trial by media.

One could name other culprits, but the current silence of the Commission for Racial Equality (CRE), the statutory body tasked with protecting ethnic minority groups from prejudice and discrimination, is scandalous. Trevor Philips' announcement of the end of multiculturalism after the Madrid bombings has again been taken up by the Right, and he recently opined that, despite the devastating picture of Muslim disadvantage in the 2001 Census, the Muslim problem is attitudinal: "too many people in this country live in the old country in their heads".[17] In Trevor's terms, Muslims "need to create a strong British Muslim identity",—that's not a problem, except that the role models he stipulates for Muslims still mentally living "back home" are Konnie Huq and Lisa Aziz.[18] How surprising it is that he misses that cornerstone of English liberalism, the personal choice to be different (and not just the same), a fact recognised by Shabina Begum's defence lawyer, Cherie Booth.[19] It seems that after the CRE failed in 2004 to incorporate the faith strand under the "race umbrella" as part of the proposed Commission for Equality and Human Rights, it has kept away from "faith" issues except in areas where it claims ownership, like "stop and search", shoot-to-kill or racial profiling, but it has not even said anything on these after 7/7.

The sheer fact of cultural diversity defines modern urban Britain, particularly the capital, and so the challenge is to reinvigorate multiculturalism by emphasizing civic responsibilities over the entitlements and rights-based approaches of the past. Another problem is the outdated compartmentalisation of policy into foreign and domestic spheres when they

[16] Sander L. Gilman, "'Barbaric' Rituals" in Susan Moller Okin et al., *Is Multiculturalism Bad for Women?* (Princeton: Princeton University Press, 1999), pp. 53–58.

[17] BBC News, 'Race Chief wants integration push', 3 April 2004, available at http://news.bbc.co.uk/1/hi/uk/3596047.stm, and *Times*, 17 July 2005.

[18] Trevor Philips, 'Why Muslims make Britain a better place', lecture at the Oxford Centre for Islamic Studies, 16 November 2004, available at http://www.cre.gov.uk/Default.aspx.LocID-0hgnew03s.RefLocID-0hg00900c002.Lang-EN.htm.

[19] The Prime Minister's wife, who is also a high-ranking lawyer, represented Begum in her legal campaign to wear the form of Islamic dress, the *jilbāb*, that she felt personally obliged to wear at the state school she attended.

so clearly now interpenetrate each other. In reaction to this blurring of sovereignties and boundaries, political retrenchments—like tribal religion and lumpen nationalism—emerge at a time of crisis, as Shaykh Hamza Yusuf bravely tried to tell British Muslims after 9/11. Are we to be a tribal umma, prepared for the sake of unity to defend Muslims, right or wrong, to ignore Muslim-on-Muslim violence, or become oblivious to general human suffering and pain?

How much is this narrowed conception of the umma held to ransom by the various expressions of Muslim nationalism, a product of post-caliphatism? In other words, is it a form of nostalgia for the imperial Ottoman model, misinterpreted as a unity based on the collective human community of monotheists, with the state re-imagined along the lines of interwar European totalitarianism? Rather it is the case, as Ibn Taymiyah and Shah Walī Allāh contended in different ways, that the umma is a body of purpose based upon the worship of God, upholding values of universal mercy and justice for all of God's creation; this, which philosophically allows for the practical recognition of multiple polities within itself, a multiplicity that is in any case an abiding fact of Muslim political history.[20] This correct attachment of purpose to the umma of purpose does not render the Muslim rootless, unanchored from the nation-state, as the philosopher Roger Scruton has contended,[21] but rather loyalties emerge from the ground up, recognised variously in the principles of moral conduct, social obligation, and contractual and legal obligations. The rights of creation (*huquq al-'ibād*) encompass family, clan, neighbourhood, city, nation, religious community and humanity, and Muslims are held to be morally and legally responsible for their fulfilment either individually or collectively.

Concomitantly, we are, as Tariq Ramadan has reminded us, a community that bears witness to the truth (*umma al-shahāda*) to all of humanity, a community that defends and establishes justice, solidarity and values of honesty, generosity, fraternity and love for all.[22] It is therefore as committed British citizens of good conscience that we may work for the common good by

[20] Naveed S. Sheikh, *The New Politics of Islam: Pan Islamic Foreign Policy in a World of States* (London: RoutledgeCurzon, 2002).

[21] Roger Scruton, *The West and the Rest: Globalization and the Terrorist Threat* (London: Continuum, 2002).

[22] Tariq Ramadan, *Western Muslims and the Future of Islam* (New York: Oxford University Press, 2004).

standing by these very principles of bearing witness to the truth, and standing up against injustice in the world and against all forms of chauvinism and self-interest. It is through this renewed vision of citizenship that British Muslims will be able to escape the perils of tribalism, to avoid becoming victims and embrace civic responsibility without surrendering their commitment to truth and justice. This renewed engagement is easily expressed in terms of the multicultural liberal democracy that has characterised Britain in recent times. This country has largely accepted that the non-recognition of cultural diversity by the state is iniquitous, and that a non-assertive secularism comfortable with faith-based activism in the public sphere is preferable to a rigid laïcité.[23] In return, new religious communities have been encouraged to undertake a civic engagement cognizant of the common good and are minimally expected to promote mutual respect and tolerance. This dispensation has now been shattered by the bombs; and for such a gross violation of deportment, deportation now looms, as 'Abdal Hakim Murad predicted some years ago.[24]

The marked weakness of the intellectual contribution by British Muslims to subsidiary debates around multiculturalism, citizenship, foreign policy objectives, civil liberties and security issues has become a critical problem. The nature of Muslim community engagement has, in the past, largely been driven by a political activism without a strong tradition of cultural and intellectual engagement, and by limited self-critical debate within the community itself. This shortfall will prove all the more telling as the national discussion oscillates between culturalist and chauvinist explanations from the Right, namely that Islam itself is the problem, and the reflex of the Left, that disaffection is explained by disadvantage. If that were the case, how could we explain the private school educations of Saajid Badat and Ahmed Omar Saeed Sheikh?

The most important point that British Muslims can make in these secondary debates on issues like multiculturalism is to insist that they cannot be completely redefined by reference to terrorism for the simple reason that

[23] For an authoritative meditation on this and other political issues facing British Muslims see Tariq Modood, *Multicultural Politics: Racism, Ethnicity and Muslims in Britain* (Edinburgh: Edinburgh University Press, 2005).

[24] 'Abdal Hakim Murad, "Tradition or Extradition? The Threat to American Muslims" in Aftab Ahmad Malik, ed., *The Empire and the Crescent: Global Implications for A New American Century* (Bristol: Amal Press, 2003) pp. 142–155.

whatever the causes of disaffection or disadvantage are among Muslim communities, there is no causal conveyor belt leading automatically to the London attacks. As the abortive attacks of 21 July (2005) demonstrate, we cannot afford to slip into the fallacy that the answers lie with cultural issues among disadvantaged Mirpuri communities in the North.[25] Whose cultural idiosyncrasies will next be found to promote Islamist extremism and violence: Somalians, African-Caribbeans or Ethiopians?[26] Problems of disaffection and disadvantage have their own provenance, which are in many ways disconnected with 7/7, and should be addressed as such, but their exploitation by opportunistic advocates of assimilation will in the current climate serve to stifle the Muslim voice, which is essential at present. So in general, the response of the Muslim communities should be to add sophistication to the national debate, to humanize it by aiding understanding of their nuanced, lived experience over the past half century in Britain, of better comprehension of the Muslim world and of the true face of their religion.

Any successful long-term strategy has to prefer a battle of theological ideas, an open, constructive debate about background causes, and a collaborative and smart intelligence-led approach to extremism. But the government may disable any such possibility by with its speedy recourse to the law, and runs the danger of creating a country where the loss of precious freedoms will not make any British citizens more secure.

POSTSCRIPT

Two years after 7/7, the search for a successful long-term strategy is still ongoing. One main reason for this is the racialisation of counter-terrorism policy in response to al-Qa'ida-type extremism, by which serious curtailments of civil liberties will not be used against the "law-abiding majority" but against "them":

> Stringent measures are possible in part because the general public does not feel vulnerable to being kept under surveillance, watching their words, being

[25] Madeleine Bunting, "Orphans of Islam", *Guardian*, 18 July 2005.

[26] Being the ethnic backgrounds of some of the other deceased suicide bombers or charged suspects associated with the attacks of 7 July and 21 July.

> arbitrarily stopped, searched, raided, beaten, arrested, or shot. By contrast, people in the Muslim and other minority communities do.[27]

Like the British Irish were in the early 1970s, British Muslims in the 2000s have been transformed into a "suspect community"[28] subject to widespread stop-and-search on the streets and at ports of entry, the internment of political prisoners, shoot-to-kill policies, house raids and hostile press coverage, which, when used too indiscriminately, is grist to the mill of extremist recruiters. In terms of politics more generally, all policy issues affecting British Muslims, e.g., education, race and equality, capacity building and mainstreaming, or foreign policy issues, have tended to be over-determined by the counter-terrorist rationales, with often deleterious consequences.

Representational Muslim politics at the national level has become more embroiled in sectarian rivalries. For a short period in 2006 and 2007, the government boycotted the Muslim Council of Britain (est. 1997), withdrawing public funding, consultation rights and public endorsement, on the basis that it was too influenced by Islamism. At the same time it has promoted the British Muslim Forum (est. 2005) and the Sufi Muslim Council (est. 2006) on the rationale that they largely represented "apolitical" British Pakistanis, Britain's largest Muslim ethnic group. This was read as valourising apolitical Sufism over Islamism, the former being seen as more compatible with an official idea of British Islam, and with the promotion of a vigorous attack against extremism, an approach exemplified by the Sufi Muslim Council.

There were also government attempts to push forward greater self-regulation of the mosque and madrasa sectors, and these efforts which were met by British Muslims with a mixture of pragmatic acceptance and suspicion.[29] More significantly the government is now also pledged to plough in 100 million pounds between 2007–2010 to build capacity in

[27] Stuart Weir, Andrew Blick and Tufyal Choudhury, *The Rules of the Game: Terrorism, Community and Human Rights* (York: Joseph Rowntree Reform Trust, 2006), p. 12.

[28] Paddy Hillyard, *Suspect Community: People's Experience of the Prevention of Terrorism Acts in Britain* (London: Pluto, 1993).

[29] Ruth Kelly, "Time for a British version of Islam", *New Statesman*, 9 April 2007. A casualty of this promotion of a Sufi-Islamist division was the carefully conceived project, the Radical Middle Way, a community-based endeavour funded by public monies, which, in its first year, sought to raise the level of mainstream theological debate around extremism, identity and belonging, integration and citizenship. Despite the quality of the project, it suffered from a cynical response about government interference and intentions. See http://www.theradicalmiddleway.co.uk.

Muslim community institutions at a local level, working through seventy local authorities, in the name of combating extremism. In the medium term, this will have a considerable impact in creating a new professional leadership with practical managerial skills to deal with underlying problems of social and economic exclusion at the Muslim grassroots.

In terms of public debate, British jihadism and Salafism have been the subject of investigative journalism and the airing of the accounts of ex-members, and, to a lesser extent, some conservative traditionalist groups like the Deobandis. Democratic Islamist groups were portrayed as politically entryist, communitarian, illiberal and even divisive whether lobbying government or making common cause with the anti-war left and using the threat of terrorism to leverage more political influence and access;[30] they were not alternatively understood as operating within the classic paradigms of liberationist identity politics developed during the 1960s.

Hizb ut-Tahrir, which has survived two reviews since 2005 on its proposed proscription under anti-terrorism legislation, has come under increasing criticism for acting as a conveyor belt towards extremism. This criticism has been articulated by ex-members in particular.[31] In all of this difficult debate there are hopeful signs that a more robust debate is emerging despite mishandled government engagement, sometimes sensationalist and inaccurate media coverage, and a widespread state of denial among too many community leaders. It is the secession of high profile convictions and the impact of large scale failed or foiled attacks over the last two years and the rising and gruesome death tolls from Iraq that have done more to lend added impetus to the national debate.

While there has been some appreciation for the strand within jihadism that stresses defending oppressed peoples,[32] there has also been considerable disquiet that much of this idealism has been systematically redirected towards targeting civilians, whether in the Muslim world or in the West. Muhammad Sidique Khan's rallying call for young British Muslims to support an ongoing Islam-West war has provided a potent macabre role model. If there were only

[30] Martin Bright, *When Progressives Treat with Reactionaries* (London: Policy Exchange, 2006).

[31] See Ed Husain, *The Islamist* (London: Penguin, 2007) and also various public interventions from Shiraz Maher and Maajid Nawaz and also Aftab Malik's chapter in this collection for further discussion on this issue.

[32] Notably Moazzam Begg, *Enemy Combatant: A British Muslim's Journey to Guantanamo and Back* (London: Free Press, 2006).

250 would-be terrorists of Muslim faith under surveillance after 9/11, that figure has increased eight-fold to around 2000 in 2007, operating in over 200 cells with some thirty plots in preparation.[33]

The debate about background causes, in the absence of an official public enquiry, has been left to sporadic interventions from politicians, community activists, journalists and academics. Unfortunately this particular debate has remained rather entrenched and has settled into recognisable silos: a widespread attack on Islamism as a form of illiberal totalitarianism and on liberal multiculturalism for fostering it; the alternate and rather embattled defence of multiculturalism and human rights; the pragmatic response that emphasises capacity building and other measures of integration; the attempt to frame the issue as one of resolving cultural values through interfaith or greater patriotism; and the insistence that seeking peace over great power politics in the Middle East would constitute the most salient response.

It is noticeable that much of this debate became thoroughly domesticated because the perpetrators of the 7/7, 21/7 and the airliner plot of August 2006 were either all British-born or British-raised. It has essentially been more an existential debate about identity and values, Muslim *and* British. The foiled plots of June 2007 on London and Glasgow demonstrated however that this form of extremism is fundamentally opportunistic and seeks to exploit weaknesses in the security system, using qualified foreign doctors in this case (who, *inter alia*, do much to help the National Health Service to run efficiently) to pursue its aims. Thus any answers as to the salience of background causes may have less to do with Britishness or multiculturalism than this debate has so far assumed.

In the past, major IRA attacks in Britain targeted civilians, soldiers and political figures, and, despite their penetration by the intelligence services in later years, the IRA retained the technical and professional resources to strike multiple targets successfully. By contrast, the "jihadi" cells seem to be comparatively amateurish, and the police, citing poor levels of intelligence penetration, claim privately to be getting lucky because of this relative lack of professionalism. The major differences between the IRA and al-Qa'ida

[33] The Prime Minister [Gordon Brown], "Statement on Security" [to the House of Commons], 25 July 2007, available at: http://www.number-10.gov.uk/output/Page12675.asp.

are that a political endgame of peace in Northern Ireland was in sight and a system of pre-attack warnings in later IRA campaigns were designed to minimize casualties. Now attacks come out of the blue and responsibility is claimed by the al-Qa'ida franchise which is not a part of a cohesive political movement that can be understood within a single national conflict as could Irish Republicanism.

The temptation in taking on a novel formation like al-Qa'ida is to frame this challenge in civilisational, even existential, terms and thus keep alive the supposition that the "war on terror" is an endless Orwellian war with no political endpoint. With two direct interventions in Afghanistan and Iraq, two proxy wars in Somalia and Lebanon, and sabre-rattling over Iran, this certainly appears to be the dismal future on offer at present.

Al-Qa'ida operates outside traditional international politics by claiming, as a non-state actor, the basic right to defend the sovereignty and autonomy of Muslim nations, a right it asserts has been forfeited by ineffectual Muslim governments. In this reading, an embryonic al-Qa'ida emerged during the early 1990s in the context of seventeen American military strikes in the Middle East between 1980 and 1995, as listed by the US State Department.[34] And while nearly all Islamists and jihadists remain nationalists, al-Qa'ida uses national or regional conflicts to advance its claim to represent the political interests of Muslims everywhere. It does not have a developed political ideology—a coherent vision of the state—but a strategy of protracted and agile guerrilla tactics heavily reliant upon Western military intervention or heightened internal suppression in the Muslim world to bolster its support. On the other hand, if al-Qa'ida has nothing more to offer than endless jihad, increasing anarchy and bloodshed and precipitating the humiliating loss of sovereignty, then it may reasonably be hoped that this misanthropic Hobbesian vision of the struggle of "all against all" will most likely burn itself out.

The solution to al-Qa'ida's strategy is disaggregating the myth of a pan-Islamic menace, instead focusing on resolving a set of local, national and regional conflicts, centred on the Middle East and West Asia. Of course that this is easier said than done, as this requires multilateral diplomacy and

[34] Mohammad-Mahmoud Mohamedou, *Understanding al-Qaeda: The Transformation of War* (London: Pluto Books, 2005).

peacemaking based on the mutual security of all the actors involved. Resolving Iraq and Israel-Palestine requires a regional peace plan based on mutual assurances of security, which needs a complete shift in emphasis from military to diplomatic measures on the part of the United States, Britain and others. It will be very difficult to enfranchise democracy and self-determination in the region without establishing this basic security and recognising the possibility of vernacular democracies in future. Of course, Britain can do very little alone, but she can still play a leading role in bringing about this transition from war to politics. The return to politics—or giving up the aspiration to remake the world in our own image in favour of living in cosmopolitan peacefulness—will be most effective counter-terrorism policy that we can mount.

2 The State We Are In

AFTAB AHMAD MALIK

WE HAVE BEEN here many times before. That same sickly feeling of disbelief that we all felt on 9/11, then again on 7/7 returned once more during the last weekend of June 2007. Like other Muslims, I too hoped and prayed that the two "Asian looking men" that crashed into the doors of the main terminal building at Glasgow airport were not Muslims, but as on 9/11 and 7/7, that hope was quickly dashed. Rather than reading about positive steps taken by Muslims to combat extremism[1] within their ranks, the week that marked the second anniversary of the 7/7 terror attacks was saturated with media reports of the failed attacks in Glasgow and London, potential new threats from al-Qa'ida and news of the sentencing of three Muslims to forty years in jail for terrorist offences. In such a climate of fear,[2] it came as no surprise then to find out that British attitudes towards Muslims have hardened.[3] The stress of being

[1] I use the term "extremism" carefully, as a Muslim looking from within his tradition. The Prophet Muhammad ﷺ said: "Beware of extremism in the religion" and the Qur'ān warns: *Commit not transgression therein, lest My anger should justly descend upon you* (20:81). Islamic terms often used to describe an imbalance in the believer are: *al-ta'assub* "being zealous or a zealot in religion", *al-ghulūw* "excessiveness, extremism", *al-tashdīd* "exceedingly restrictive" and *al-tatarruf* "moving to the farthest point". All these words basically signify a tendency away from what is deemed moderate and balanced.

[2] In a recent case concerning a suspected Muslim suicide bomber, jury members were asked "not to convict the accused through a 'fear or alarm' of Islam". See "Terror Jury Islamophobia Warning", BBC News http://news.bbc.co.uk/1/hi/scotland/tayside_and_central/6991074.stm.

[3] That is, as compared to other European nations. See the Harris poll: http://www.harrisinteractive.com/harris_poll/index.asp?PID=801. It also appears that our transatlantic cousins are not faring too well either. A USA Today/Gallup Poll conducted in 2006 found that one in five Americans said that they would not want a Muslim for a neighbour and a whopping 40 percent supported mandatory identification cards for Muslims living in America. Cf., Hazem Kira, "Un-Wholly America", *Illume Magazine*, http://www.illumemedia.org/artman/publish/article_648.php

viewed as a fifth column, a whole series of highly publicised terror raids across the country, generalisations and stereotyping[4] (and the need to continually respond to such stereotypes) has taken its toll on Muslims, who increasingly view the war on terrorism as the first stage of a wider plan to undermine and attack the Muslim way of life. Everything from the way a Muslim dresses to which mosque he might visit[5] have been scrutinized and analysed and a tell-tale formula has been produced to show which Muslims are most likely to be extremists.[6] No stone has been left unturned and there is little sanctity or refuge for Muslims from the public and media glare. A siege mentality has sunk in, creating a defensive refusal to acknowledge and face challenges.[7] The Muslim population has come to see an elite that is determined to initiate an "Islamic reformation", to tell Muslims what is and is not "moderate" Islam and what is and is not good for them.

THE CONSPIRACY DEEPENS

Two years after the 7/7 attacks, a survey of five hundred British Muslims revealed that nearly a quarter believed the British government had

[4] "Public opinion surveys in the United States and Europe show that nearly half of Westerners associate Islam with violence and Muslims with terrorists". Kenneth Ballen, "The Myth of Muslim Support for Terror", *Christian Science Monitor*, February 23, 2007 http://www.csmonitor.com/2007/0223/p09s01-coop.html.

[5] A recent example of this was a series of articles that appeared in the *Times* (September 7 and September 10, 2007) that cast the Deobandis (a revivalist movement founded in India in 1867, that has a considerable following in the UK) vis-à-vis one of their popular and outspoken imams, Abu Yusuf Riyadh al-Haq, as extremists. Warning about the "Hard line takeover of British mosques" that wish to "convert all Britain" and focusing particularly on Riyadh al-Haq ("the home grown cleric who loathes the British") the newspaper urged that "British Muslims should recognize the threat of Deobandi extremism". Muslims generally saw this as an outlandish scare-tactic to persuade the public that there is an immediate and home grown threat from a major segment of the Muslim population. While one might take considerable objection to some of the opinions of Shaykh Riyadh al-Haq, to portray him as the representative, or the spiritual inheritor of the Deobandis in the United Kingdom is disingenuous. This "revelation" followed on from a slew of television documentaries that sought to unveil the "extremist threat" and messages of hate being perpetuated by so called "mainstream" mosques in Britain.

[6] For example, see Stephen Schwartz, "As an American Muslim, I warn you: Britain has a unique problem," *Spectator*, pp. 14–15, vol. 301, no. 9288; and my reply: "As a British Muslim, I advise you: Don't be alarmed by Stephen Schwartz", http://www.amalpress.com/events/schwartz_British_Muslim.pdf.

[7] See, for example, how radical groups prey on the state of denial for recruiting to their cause in Hassan Butt, "Muslim heads stuck firmly in the sand", *Times Online*, July 14, 2007 http://www.timesonline.co.uk/tol/comment/columnists/guest_contributors/article2072587.ece.

some involvement with the 7/7 terror attacks and that in fact, the four suicide bombers were not responsible.[8] This survey demonstrates the growing alienation and distrust many Muslims have of the British government. Conspiracies tend to emerge when people begin to doubt the official narrative and certainly, the sceptics do have a lot to be sceptical about. The fact that the government is unwilling to carry out an independent public inquiry into the 7/7 terror attacks seems to confirm to this nearly 25 percent of Muslims that the government indeed has something to hide.

Conspiracy theories are not unique to Muslims. Popular conspiracy theories over 9/11 have found a larger audience with non-Muslims. A poll conducted in August 2006 found that 36 percent of Americans considered it "'very likely' or 'somewhat likely' that government officials either allowed the attacks to be carried out or carried out the attacks themselves".[9] This is a significant number and should not merely be dismissed as a fringe opinion, but rather "[i]t is a mainstream political reality" that also says a great deal about the trust Americans have in their government.[10]

This conspiracy-theory mentality leaves Muslims in a quandary. There are Muslims (albeit a fringe minority) who on 9/11, actually celebrated this act of wanton terror, calling the nineteen hijackers the "magnificent nineteen" and referring to those who carried out the 7/7 attacks as "knights". Thus on the one hand, the Muslim community must face those who refuse to believe that Muslims are capable of such destruction, and on the other hand, address the reality that there is "an unchallenged, unreported Islamist underworld in which talk of jihad, bombings, stabbings, killings, and executions are the norm".[11]

[8] Mark Tran, "Poll: Government had a Role in July 7 Bombings", *Guardian Unlimited* http://politics.guardian.co.uk/terrorism/story/0,,2095752,00.html?gusrc=rss&feed=19.

[9] Lev Grossman "Why the 9/11 Conspiracy Theories Won't Go Away", *Time*, http://www.time.com/time/printout/0,8816,1531304,00.html.

[10] A recent Zogby poll reveals that 51 percent of Americans support a new congressional enquiry into President Bush's and Vice President Dick Cheney's role before, during and after the 9/11 attacks; 30 percent support the immediate impeachment of both and 67 percent say the 9/11 Commission should have investigated the still unexplained collapse of Building 7 (which was announced to the media 30 minutes before it fell symmetrically to the ground at freefall speed). Previous polls have found that fewer than 20 percent of Americans believe they have been told the full story of the 9/11 attacks. See http://www.911truth.org/images/ZogbyPoll2007.pdf.

[11] Ed Hussain, "Books, Betrayals, and Beheadings", *New Statesman*, June 18, 2006, p. 18.

ANGER

Writing in his diary, the twenty-six year old British jihadi Zeeshan Siddiqui often noted that when he was feeling down, he would "*entertain* himself with violent jihadi videos, or the news". Having read his diary, Dominic Casciani concludes that quite clearly "what emerges is an exceptionally troubled young man consumed with anger".[12] And what propels this anger? If there was any doubt before, there is now no shortage of evidence to substantiate the correlation between foreign policy and so called Muslim rage.[13]

In a world of 24 hour news coverage of unfolding events, beamed into homes or made available through the Internet, Muslims are bombarded with images that instil guilt and create a sense of powerlessness, a complete inability to help fellow Muslims against the onslaught of "Zionist forces", and "Crusader Americans". From the relentless bombing of Afghanistan to the masquerade that led to the invasion of Iraq and the ensuing chaos and violence; from the destruction of ancient mosques in the city of Fallujah to the Friday raid at the Abu Hanifa Mosque in Baghdad; from the "enemy combatants" held at Guantanamo Bay in limbo, without charge, trial or access to counsel, to the dehumanising pictures of abuse at Abu Ghuraib; from the killing of the wounded Iraqi by a US Marine, captured forever on television, to the 655,000[14] "collaterally" killed Muslim men, women and children in Iraq, the reality of the war on terrorism has become crystal clear: Muslims are being humiliated, their blood is cheap and Islam itself is under siege. In this state where primal emotions determine actions, anger quickly emerges in the Muslim psyche. Make no mistake; this anger is real. In the inner cities of Birmingham, East London, Luton, Bradford and elsewhere, its intensity is palpable.

[12] Emphasis added. Dominic Casciani, "Jihadi Diary: Inside the Mind", BBC News, http://news.bbc.co.uk/2/hi/uk_news/magazine/6750911.stm.

[13] See: Vikram Dodd, "Police Report: Foreign Policy Helped Make UK a Target", *Guardian*, July 7, 2006, http://www.guardian.co.uk/attackonlondon/story/0,,1814756,00.html.

[14] This figure was 100,000 when this essay was first written in 2006 and was the conclusion of a survey conducted by the British medical journal, *Lancet*. See David Brown, "Study Claims Iraq's 'Excess' Death Toll Has Reached 655,000", *Washington Post*, http://www.washingtonpost.com/wp-dyn/content/article/2006/10/10/AR2006101001442_pf.html

The catalyst for the radicalisation[15] of Muslims did not begin with the war on terrorism—this has only served to accelerate it. It was simmering long before 9/11. The single galvanizing issue has always been Palestine. I know this to be true with deadly accuracy. In December 2001, after delivering a lecture about the development of Islamic scholarship, I soon found myself being asked questions about suicide bombing missions. One individual in particular had great difficulty in understanding why traditional Muslim scholars specifically rejected such missions in Israel where Muslims had been made refugees and were being oppressed and humiliated on a daily basis. The individual was none other than Asif Mohammed Hanif. Those who knew him say that he was a gentle giant, a considerate, quiet individual who helped his family and others, characteristics also shared by the 7/7 suicide bombers. In Asif's case, his concern over Palestine was manipulated with deadly effect. The same concern played a pivotal role, along with Iraq and Afghanistan, in driving the 7/7 suicide bombers to their destructive ends.[16]

LOOKING WITHIN

But is it really as simple as blaming foreign policy for Muslim extremism? (Muslims don't have a monopoly on anger over foreign policy, so how do

[15] Radicalisation does not simply mean "politicisation". Rather, it is the *corruption* of Islamic law and theology, which is then used to justify any means to achieve the creation of an Islamic state. Throughout this chapter, "radical" is used in conjunction with Islamist (see note 17 for definition). Radical Islamists are highly politicised individuals who work outside of the democratic process for the creation of an Islamic state. They morally justify the attacks of 9/11, are quick to excommunicate other Muslims (*takfir*), encourage a militant jihad (that is, they follow a jihad doctrine that is not grounded in traditional Islamic law or theology) and pursue a literalist doctrine. Radical Islamists are a very small fringe within the broad definition of "Islamism". While every radical is an extremist, not every extremist is a radical.

[16] See Daniel McGroy and Micheal Theodoulou, "Suicide Bomber's Video Confession Blames Iraq War", *Times Online*, http://www.timesonline.co.uk/tol/news/uk/article561829.ece. For the actual transcript of Muhammad Sidique Khan (referred to as the ringleader of the 7/7 bombers) see http://news.bbc.co.uk/1/hi/uk/4206800.stm. The recording of this video was also accompanied by a message from Ayman al-Zawahiri who cites the London attacks in reciprocity for the invasion of Muslim lands; "After centuries of invading our land and occupying it ... this is for you to taste some of what you have made us taste before". See Phil Hirschkorn and David Ensor, "U.S., UK Investigate 'Bomber Tape'", CNN.COM, http://www.cnn.com/2005/WORLD/europe/09/02/london.claim/. Whereas Khan does not specifically mention Afghanistan, Iraq or Palestine, he does refer to the "atrocities [committed] against my people all over the world". However Zawahiri, in his message, specifically mentions "the aggression against Palestine, Iraq, and Afghanistan". See Paul Reynolds, "Bomber Video 'Points to al-Qaeda'", BBC News, http://news.bbc.co.uk/1/hi/uk/4208250.stm.

we account for the fact that we have yet to see non-Muslims so enraged that they become suicide bombers?) Not so, according to British ex-Islamists[17] such as Ed Husain, Hassan Butt and Maajid Nawaz,[18] who have all stressed the corruption of traditional Islamic values and their consequent replacement by a highly political reading of Islam. They are uniquely qualified to speak on this issue, because they propagated and recruited others to it.[19] "By blaming the government for our actions, those who pushed the 'Blair's bombs' line did our propaganda work for us", wrote Butt.[20] "More important, they also helped to draw away any critical examination from the real engine of our violence: Islamic theology". Butt, who was a recruiter to what he calls the "British Jihadi Network" knows well and at first hand how in radical circles the entire world is seen *dār al-kufr* (the abode of unbelief) in which Muslims have an obligation to fight unbelief, and so by extension, to wage war against the whole world. With this skewered reading—one that departs from traditional Islam—radicals

[17] The word Islamist has been defined in different ways by various academics and analysts, and this has led to some confusion when this word is invoked. There is the broad definition that distinguishes its usage from Shiite Islamism. In this context, it is seen as synonymous with Sunni "Islamic activism", encapsulating three broad manifestations: political; missionary; and jihadi. By and large, political Islamists work within the confines of the nation-state and use democratic means to bring about change. Missionary Islamists (sometimes referred to as "fundamentalists") are confined to self-rectification, a focus on doctrine and are generally apolitical. Jihadists are further subdivided into those who fight local 'corrupt' rulers; those who fight (typically) non-Muslim invaders of Muslim lands (the "near enemy") and those who advocate a "global" jihad, namely against the West, and the United States in particular (the "far enemy").

The word has also been used haphazardly to include both Sunni and Shiite manifestations in which it is seen to be synonymous with a "threat" and/or "menace" to western values/interests. The term is sometimes used along with "extremist" and "radical" to acknowledge that Islamism itself is a diverse term and is prefaced by such words to describe those Islamists that oppose democracy, seek the establishment of an Islamic state and justify violence against civilians in order to achieve political aims. In using "Islamists" throughout this essay, I use it in a narrow sense; to describe highly politicised twentieth-century revivalist movements with essentialist interpretations of Islam, who advocate a return to the caliphate. In doing so, they often contravene well-established interpretations within Islam's scholarly tradition.

[18] See Ed Husain, *The Islamist: Why I Joined Radical Islam in Britain, What I Saw Inside and Why I Left* (London: Penguin, 2007); for the views of Hassan Butt prior to his reform, see: "A British Jihadist", in *Prospect* #113 (August 2005), pp.18–24 and for his views now, refer to note 20; Maajid Nawaz has his own blog in which he aims to address some of the legal and theological flaws of Hizb ut-Tahrir (also see note 27) www.maajidnawaz.blogspot.com.

[19] Inayat Bunglawala of the MCB (Muslim Council of Britain) however urges some caution at what advice such ex-Islamists may be offering (see http://commentisfree.guardian.co.uk/inayat_bunglawala/2007/06/seeing_the_light.html) and he isn't alone. See note 83.

[20] Hassan Butt, "My Plea to Fellow Muslims: You Must Renounce Terror", *Observer*, July 1, 2007, http://www.guardian.co.uk:80/commentisfree/story/0,,2115891,00.html.

are given the green light "to destroy the sanctity of the five rights that every human is granted under Islam: life, wealth, land, mind and belief. In *dār al-ḥarb* [the abode of war], anything goes, including the treachery and cowardice of attacking civilians". Hassan Butt's contention however, is that Muslims cannot ignore "those passages of the Koran which instruct on killing unbelievers". This indicates that Butt has yet to free himself from the literalist reading that he employed as a radical, and expose himself to the rich and early commentary works on both the Prophetic traditions (*ḥadīth*) and the Qur'ān. Such passages that are commonly used to justify killing innocents are discussed in both David Dakake's and Shaykh Afifi's contributions to this volume as well as in Zaid Shakir's essay, "Jihad as Perpetual War".[21] While one cannot deny that there are opinions within the vast Islamic corpus of Islamic jurisprudence that do justify violence, these opinions have never been embraced by the Muslim world as normative. Rather, there is a far greater, richer and diverse corpus of work that offers alternative readings that repudiate such understandings. Butt also mentions that the Muslim scholars demarcated the world into "the abode of war" and "the abode of peace", which is true only to an extent. The Qur'ān itself does not make mention of these two abodes and Khaled Abou El Fadl points to the historical context within which this juristic formulation came about. He also points to the fact that even during the medieval period treatises of non-belligerence were signed between Muslims and non-Muslims. Furthermore, jurists soon after coined a third category, that of the abode of neutrality (*dār al-sulḥ* or *al-'aḥd*) and so they stopped viewing the world in bi-polar terms as it became increasingly complex and interdependent, and as large groups of Muslims migrated to traditionally non-Muslim lands. In short, El Fadl argues that these abodes were thoroughly a product of historical circumstances, not an article of faith, as radicals assume.[22]

[21] In Aftab Ahmad Malik, ed., *The Empire and the Crescent: Global Implications for a New American Century* (Bristol: Amal Press, 2003). Also see Sherman Jackson, "Jihad in the Modern World", *Journal of Islamic Law and Culture* (Spring/Summer, 2002).

[22] See Khaled Abou El Fadl, *The Great Threat: Wrestling Islam from the Extremists* (New York: Harper Collins, 2005), pp. 224–232. For a re-examination of the notions of the abode of Islam and the abode of unbelief by a former Islamist, and the understanding of early Muslim scholars on the abode of Islam, see: Maajid Nawaz, "Evaluating Hizb ut-Tahrir's Theo-political Stance," on his blog: http://maajidnawaz.blogspot.com/2007/08/evaluating-hizbut-tahrirs-theo.html.

In *The Islamist*, Ed Husain provides a firsthand account into the thoughts and attitudes of an Islamist's worldview; one that is very much demarcated along religious lines, always clear cut, always has answers and is unambiguous. This simplified worldview allows the individual to quickly differentiate between "good" and "bad" Muslims. It presupposes that all non-Muslims are inferior to Muslims and by doing so, strips most of humanity of their dignity. To assert one's "Britishness" was akin to negating one's "Muslimness", as the two are mutually exclusive. Participation in the political process is strictly prohibited (*ḥarām*) and tantamount to apostasy. Thus, with a self-perpetuating polarized worldview, these Muslims retreat from society, creating their own subculture in which all non-Muslims are simply referred to as *kuffār*.[23] It is natural then for radicals to see themselves as the exclusive inheritors of God's (unpolluted) message, in which they are viewed as chosen agents for bringing change to an ungodly world. Any offence to them is in effect an offence against God, who is viewed as "full of vengeance, a legislator, a controller, [and] a punisher". This path, treaded only by the elite, is liberating. It fully empowers the individual to choose how to live, how to worship[24] and even who to marry,[25] squarely challenging established cultural norms.[26] In this atmosphere, local challenges faced by Muslims are connected to an international conspiracy against Islam. The ineptitude of Muslims to confront and solve challenges is deemed to be only remedied through seizing political power. The discourse is one which, to a large extent, marginalises any ethical and moral discourse. The virtue of patience is seen as a vice; misplaced in a time that demands action. The problem is that in their patchwork

[23] As expected, this classification is a fundamental departure from traditional Islam. The Qur'ān categorises creation in three groups: believers (Muslims) non-Muslims (*kuffār*) and humankind (*nās*). Christians and Jews are honoured as *ahl al-kitāb* (People of the Book); inheritors of a divine message. For further details on the dignity of the "other" in Islamic discourse, refer to Hashim Kamali, *The Dignity of Man: An Islamic Perspective* (Cambridge: Islamic Texts Society, 2001).

[24] Husain notes that as his "Islamic" activism increased, his "relationship with God had deteriorated". He also notes that while recruits were quick to deconstruct various systems and articulate the supremacy of the Islamic political system, most could barely recite the Qur'ān or were "clueless" when it came to basic aspects of worship and etiquette. See *The Islamist*.

[25] Butt contends that Muhammad Sidique Khan told him that he was first drawn to "radical Islam" because it offered him a way out of a traditional arranged marriage. See Butt's interview on 60 Minutes http://youtube.com/watch?v=odr2pJeSMqU.

[26] For example, see Shiv Malik, "The Making of a Terrorist: The Inside Story of 7/7 Leader Muhammad Sidique Khan", *Prospect* #135 (June 2007).

approach to understanding the world today, these individuals ignore the complexities and nuances of Islamic scholarship, which vanish as a simple and comforting worldview is constructed for Muslims. It is a black and white world, one that has no need for beauty, diversity or colour.

Husain and Nawaz, both former members of Hizb ut-Tahrir have explained its pursuit of a political theology that makes no exceptions or compromises to achieve its political doctrine. Hizb ut-Tahrir is engaged in an ideological struggle for the restoration of the Islamic state, or caliphate. While it condemns violence and terrorism, and has distinctly "progressed" since the days when its British leadership was under Omar Bakri Muhammad, it has been argued that the group nonetheless fosters a climate of hate and intolerance. It was founded by Taqi al-Din al-Nabahani (d. 1979), a Palestinian judge who sought to unite the Muslim world against western neo-colonialism through the restoration of the caliphate. Both Husain and Nawaz argue that Hizb ut-Tahrir departs from traditional Islamic legal thought and theology by viewing the entire world as *dār al-kufr* (the abode of unbelief). They readily excommunicate Muslim rulers for not implementing or ruling by God's law which they view as a heresy corrected only by force. It then becomes an obligation for Muslims to declare war against such rulers. However, the definition of *dār al-Islām* and *dār al-ḥarb* has varied over the centuries and by ignoring (or even acknowledging) this plurality of opinions, Hizb ut-Tahrir projects theirs as a universally accepted and binding definition.

Nawaz, citing core party texts, points to the fact that the establishment of the Islamic state under the auspices of Hizb ut-Tahrir would bring with it new levels of violence, as it not only justifies "killing millions of Muslims" to unify all Muslim countries into a single state but also "killing every apostate even if they numbered millions". Indeed, violence is not ruled out for its establishment, since Hizb ut-Tahrir believes that all current Muslim governments must be overthrown to make way for a single, unified caliphate.[27] Islam is thus transformed into "a narrow political

[27] For a critique of the theological outlook of Hizb ut-Tahrir, see: Zeyno Baran, ed., *The Challenge of Hizb ut-Tahrir: Deciphering and Combating Radical Islamist Ideology* (Nixon Center, 2004), http://www.nixoncenter.org/Program%20Briefs/PB%202004/confrephiztahrir.pdf. For a more scholarly and academic, yet brief overview, see Jean-Francois Mayer, *Hizb ut-Tahrir: The Next Al-Qaeda, Really?* (Federal Department of Foreign Affairs [DFA] Political Affairs Division IV, Geneva, 2004), http://hei.unige.ch/psio/fichiers/Meyer%20Al%20Qaida.pdf. For a thorough and scholarly analysis of

ideology",[28] which then preys upon "the anger and confusion of young British Muslim men",[29] that is so often triggered in times of crisis.

In short, all three ex-Islamists point to the destructive consequences of nurturing a theology of hate that is justified by Islamic vocabulary and texts. But how are such ideas able to spread and gain popularity? While the primary source for guidance in the Muslim community is the imam, it has been noted that only six percent speak English as their first language,[30] so who else can young Muslims turn to? Left with little choice and many questions, the most accessible source for answers is the Internet, which has quickly become a fertile ground for the nurture and spread of doctrinal distortions and the democratisation of *ijtihād*,[31] thereby effectively vesting anyone, regardless of age, education, rationality or piety, the competence to be a jurist. The Internet has compounded this problem, as ill-informed opinions are termed fatwas,[32] and presented as if written by scholarly authorities.[33]

Firmly placed within their circumstances—high levels of unemployment,[34] increasing feelings of alienation from a society that is perceived as waging war on Islam, in which "[d]istrust, fear and even hatred of anything Islamic

the movement, refer to Suha Taji-Farouki, *A Fundamental Quest: Hizb al-Tahir and the Search for the Islamic Caliphate* (London: Grey Seal, 1996). A draft constitution of the caliphate as understood by Hizb ut-Tahrir is included in the book but is also available online: http://www.hizb-ut-tahrir.info/english/constitution.htm. For a brief yet erudite discussion on the historicity of the caliphate, see: Khalid Yahya Blankinship, *The History of the Caliphate* (Lamppost Productions), http://lamppostproductions.org/index.php?option=com_content&task=view&id=17&Itemid=39

[28] Peter Baumont, "Leading Militant in Split with Islamists", *Observer*, September 9, 2007, http://observer.guardian.co.uk/uk_news/story/0,,2165439,00.html.

[29] Jane Perlez, "Ex-radical turns to Islam of tolerance", *International Herald Tribune Europe*, June 1, 2007, http://www.iht.com/articles/2007/06/01/news/profile.php?page=1.

[30] Richard Holt, "Only 6pc of Imams Are Native English speakers", *Telegraph*, 6 July 2007, http://www.telegraph.co.uk/news/main.jhtml?xml=/news/2007/07/06/nislam106.xml.

[31] Literally, "striving". A scholarly endeavour; competence to infer expert legal rulings from foundational proofs within or without a particular school of law.

[32] A fatwa is a juristic legal opinion that is *not* binding. The key word here is juristic. One needs to be a qualified expert (a mufti) and grounded in all the requisite sciences to present a valid fatwa.

[33] For an authoritative reading of the general impact of the Internet on the Muslim appreciation of knowledge and the emergence of online fatwas and "E-Jihad" specifically, see Gary Bunt, *Virtually Islamic: Computer-mediated Communication and Cyber Islamic Environments* (Wales: University of Wales Press, 2002) and Gary Bunt, *Islam in the Digital Age: E-Jihad, Online* Fatwas *and Cyber Islamic Environments* (London: Pluto Press, 2003).

[34] Statistics reveal that when compared to other faith groups, Muslims have the highest unemployment rates. Rates of unemployment are highest for Muslims between the ages of 16 and 24. See http://www.statistics.gov.uk/cci/nugget.asp?id=979.

is not uncommon",[35] it is quite easy to see why such messages might resonate with young Muslims. The message is anti-establishment; it serves as a form of protest against the unfair application and administration of justice; it offers an identity that brings with it security, a purpose and a sense of belonging.[36] The void created by the erosion of traditional Islam, which is viewed by second and third generation Muslims as at best pietistic and at worst misguided, is filled with an activism that is characterised by spiritual arrogance. In this void, young Muslims search for simple and immediate answers. It is as if they no longer need years of serious theological and legal studies, their truth is determined by personal experience and emotion. They have no need to consult learned scholars when they can go directly to the Qur'ān and the ḥadīth; their souls lie ignored as they become more concerned with outward matters, until eventually they are unable to recognise the symptoms of their diseased and dying hearts.

THE POLITICS OF THE "WAR ON TERROR": IGNORING THE OBVIOUS

"Just why do terrorists terrorise?" asks Bill Blum, author of *Rogue State* and *Killing Hope*. We have been told time and time again that these terrorists simply "hate our freedoms", and that is all that motivates them. However, Graham E. Fuller,[37] the former vice-chairman of the National Intelligence Council at the CIA, along with other officials, think-tanks and journalists,

[35] Douglas Blane, "New Teachings on Islamophobia", *Times Educational Supplement*, September 14, 2007, http://www.tes.co.uk/2431112. The EU race watchdog, The European Monitoring Centre on Racism and Xenophobia (EUMC), reported that anti-Islamic feeling has "detonated" in the UK since 2001. For a thorough catalogue of the impact of 9/11 on Muslims living in Britain, see "Anti-Islamic reactions in the EU after the terrorist acts against the US", http://eumc.eu.int/eumc/material/pub/anti-islam/collection/UK.pdf. This report looks at the period from 12 September to 31 December 2001. Following the 7 July bombings in 2005, it was reported that religious hate crimes rose six-fold in London and were directed mostly against Muslims. The media's discourse on Islam has been saturated with a variety of anti-Muslim terminology, such as: "Islamic fascism", "Islamic extremism" and "Islamist terrorism", such that many Muslims see this as open season on Islam and Muslims.

[36] Nawaz mentions that when he was sixteen years old his first encounter with a member from Hizb ut-Tahrir was one in which the latter "preyed on his confusion about his British Pakistani identity". See Jane Perlez, "From Finding Radical Islam to Losing an Ideology", *New York Times* (Europe) September 12, 2007, http://www.nytimes.com/2007/09/12/world/europe/12britain.html?_r=1&n=Top/Reference/Times%20Topics/People/P/Perlez,%20Jane&oref=slogin.

[37] Graham E. Fuller, "Muslims Abhor the Double Standard", *Los Angeles Times*, 5 October 2001.

has long repudiated such an assertion.[38] Zbigniew Brzezinski, national security advisor during the Carter administration, in a CNN interview came straight to the point when he asked candidly: "[W]e have to ask ourselves, what fuels them? What sustains them? What produces the terrorists?" His answer: "Political rage over a number of issues". Michael Scheuer, the former Bin Laden Unit Chief at the CIA and the author of *Imperial Hubris*, noted that "this war has nothing to do with who we are or what we believe, and everything to do with what we do in the Islamic world". In other words, "the motivation for the people fighting us has to do with our policies".[39] One does not need to be a rocket scientist to figure out what the motivations of the terrorists are, when they have consistently stated them in the clearest terms. As Blum clearly demonstrates:

> The terrorists responsible for the bombing of the World Trade Centre in 1993 sent a letter to the *New York Times* which stated, in part: "We declare our responsibility for the explosion on the mentioned building. This action was done in response for the American political, economical, and military support to Israel the state of terrorism and to the rest of the dictator countries in the region".
>
> Richard Reid, who tried to ignite a bomb in his shoe while aboard an American Airline flight to Miami in December 2001, told police that his planned suicide attack was an attempt to strike a blow against the US campaign in Afghanistan and the Western economy. In an e-mail sent to his mother, which he intended her to read after his death, Reid wrote that it was his duty "to help remove the oppressive American forces from the Muslims land".
>
> After the bombings in Bali, one of the leading suspects—later convicted—told police that the bombings were "revenge" for "what Americans have done to Muslims". He said that he wanted to "kill as many Americans as possible" because "America oppresses the Muslims".
>
> In November 2002, a taped message from Osama bin Laden began: "The road to safety begins by ending the aggression. Reciprocal treatment is part of justice. The [terrorist] incidents that have taken place [...] are only reactions and reciprocal actions".
>
> That same month, when Mir Aimal Kasi, who killed several people outside of CIA headquarters in 1993, was on death row, he declared: "What

[38] See "Why Do They Hate Us?" in Aftab Ahmad Malik, ed., *With God on Our Side: Politics and Theology of the War on Terrorism* (Bristol: Amal Press, 2005).

[39] See his interview with Buzzflash: http://www.buzzflash.com/interviews/05/01/int05001.html.

> I did was a retaliation against the US government" for American policy in the Middle East and its support of Israel.[40]

Vocal calls for reform from non-Muslims in the West serve only to fuel the terrorists' claim that what the West really wants, and has always wanted, is a new "approved" version of Islam: one that has been rubber-stamped by the neo-conservatives and their associated think-tanks. The fact that the American government is spending billions of dollars in an attempt to "change the face of Islam" to bring about an "Islamic reformation", feeds directly into the hands of conspiracy theorists and the fanatical fringe. The *US News*, citing a classified document, reported that "the US has a national security interest in *influencing* what happens *within* Islam".[41] Even before the invasion of Iraq, then Deputy of Defense Secretary Paul Wolfowitz proclaimed that "We need an Islamic reformation". His sentiments have been echoed by Daniel Pipes, who declared that the "'ultimate goal' of the war on terrorism had to be Islam's modernisation, or, 'religion-building'".[42]

It is no wonder that since the unfolding of the war on terrorism, concerns abound that the fearful days of colonial domination are back again. The lessons learned from colonialism, when Muslims became uprooted from their tradition through attempts to "modernize" and "reform" Islam, have undoubtedly contributed to the making of the very terrorists that the US administration and the British government[43] are

[40] Cf., Bill Blum, "Myth and Denial in the War on Terrorism: Just Why do Terrorists Terrorize?" in *With God on Our Side*, p. 109.

[41] Emphasis added. See David E. Kaplan, "Hearts, Minds, and Dollars in an Unseen Front in the War on Terrorism, America is Spending Millions... To Change the Very Face of Islam", USNews.com, http://www.usnews.com/usnews/news/articles/050425/25roots.htm.

[42] See Jim Lobe, "From Iraqi Occupation to Islamic Reformation: Neo-cons Aim Beyond Baghdad", *Foreign Policy in Focus*. http://www.fpif.org/commentary/2004/0404neocons_body.html.

[43] On 27 June 2007, after receiving overwhelming backing by Labour MPs, Gordon Brown replaced Tony Blair as Prime Minister. Despite his support of Tony Blair's war strategy, there is hope that as Prime Minister, Brown will make a concerted effort to move away from the disastrous foreign policy pursuits of the Blair era. There is a genuine opportunity to win back disaffected Labour supporters and earn respect from the Muslim community, by signalling a new spirit of engagement with the Muslim world. But this will take courage and an immense amount of political will. Although still early, the signs so far are promising: the Prime Minister has spoken about "learning lessons" from Iraq (although, as rightly noted, he did not mention *what* those lessons were); and the new foreign secretary, David Miliband, recently acknowledged that British foreign policy had alienated millions of Muslims, who perceive that Britain seeks only to dominate them, rather than empower them. Gordon Brown has also been quick to distance himself from the euphemism that gives credence to the belief

waging war against today. Many Muslims also see the recommendations and strategies suggested in "Civil Democratic Islam",[44] the RAND report that suggests ways of combating Muslim extremism (by effectively setting up a clash between "moderate" and "extremist" Muslims) unfolding on a daily basis and have become extremely wary of any government-led initiatives to combat extremism, lest they become pawns in a greater game.

While both the US administration and the British government are determined to continue this war on terrorism, which Donald Rumsfeld called "sustained, comprehensive and unrelenting", they tragically continue to ignore a principle cause of Muslim radicalisation. The rejection of any link between the UK's foreign policy towards Iraq and the 7/7 bombings[45] will not only increase distrust of the government's motives in the war on terrorism, but it is also contrary to reports from the intelligence services.[46] As early as 2003, the Joint Intelligence Committee (which oversees the security services) "assessed that al-Qa'ida and associated groups continued to represent by far the greatest terrorist threat

that the war on terrorism is a war on Islam; he has moved swiftly to stop ministers from using "Muslim" in connection with terrorism. Indeed, the phrase "war on terror" has been dropped from the lexicon of the new government. Speaking at his first conference with President Bush at Camp David, Bush reminded the world that the West was confronting "an ideology of darkness", whereas Brown emphasized that "terrorism is not a cause; it is a crime". He went further to express that the conflict was not with "terror", but with "al-Qa'ida-inspired terrorism". Following the meeting, a headline in the *Washington Post* declared that Brown was "More bulldog than poodle". It appears that Brown will not play ball as did his predecessor, but has a new philosophy in dealing with the conflict against radical Islamism in which his first step as Prime Minister is to win the hearts and minds of Muslims.

[44] Cheryl Benard, "Civil Democratic Islam: Partners, Resources, and Strategies", RAND Corporation http://www.rand.org/pubs/monograph_reports/2005/MR1716.pdf.

[45] Then Prime Minister Tony Blair remarked that the 7/7 attacks were "a form of terrorism aimed at our way of life, not at any particular Government or policy". See the transcript of the Prime Minister's speech concerning the 7/7 London attacks, available from http://www.parliament.the-stationery-office.co.uk/pa/cm200506/cmhansrd/cm050711/debtext/50711-09.htm.

[46] Let us also not forget that a poll conducted in 2003 revealed that "79 percent of Londoners felt that British forces involvement in an attack on Iraq would make a terrorist attack on London more likely". See "Londoners to Quiz Mayoral Candidates on War, Occupation and the Impact on London", Press Release by CND, 19 May 2004. http://www.cnduk.org/pages/press/190504.html. Following the terror attack on London, the *Guardian* published a poll that stated "Two-thirds of Britons believe there is a link between Tony Blair's decision to invade Iraq and the London bombings despite government claims to the contrary". See Julian Glover, "Two-thirds Believe London Bombings are Linked to Iraq", *Guardian Unlimited*, July 19, 2005. http://www.guardian.co.uk/attackonlondon/story/0,16132,1531387,00.html.

to Western interests, and that threat would be heightened by military action against Iraq".[47] Following the train bombings in Madrid in 2004, a Home Office and Foreign Office dossier, ordered by then Prime Minister Tony Blair, identified Iraq as a "recruiting sergeant" for extremism. The report clearly acknowledged that "a particularly strong cause of disillusionment among Muslims, including young Muslims, is a perceived 'double standard'" that arises from "the foreign policy of western governments, in particular Britain and the US".[48] Only weeks before the 7/7 attacks, we were informed that "[h]igh-ranking security and intelligence officials warned [...] that the war in Iraq had increased the risk of terrorism in Britain [...]".[49] The *Guardian*, printing information from a leaked report by the Joint Terrorist Analysis Centre that includes officials from MI5, MI6, GCHQ and the police "explicitly linked US-led involvement in Iraq with terrorist activity in the UK [...]".[50] In the United States, a report by the influential Defense Science Board, which advises the Secretary of Defense, Deputy Secretary of Defense and the Chairman of the Joint Chiefs of Staff, acknowledged in 2004 that "Muslims do not hate our freedom, but rather they hate our policies". The report warned that "No public relations campaign can save America from flawed policies".[51]

THE WAR OF ERROR

A recent world poll by Gallup concludes that the Cold War paradigm that current US policy makers are using to define their war is flawed. The Cold War was a battle for the supremacy of a worldview, namely communism or democracy; policymakers now believe communism has been replaced

[47] See George Jones, "Blair Rejected Terror Warnings", *Telegraph*. http://www.telegraph.co.uk/news/main.jhtml?xml=/news/2003/09/12/ndoss12.xml&sSheet=/news/2003/09/12/ixnewstop.html.

[48] Robert Winnett and David Leppard, "Leaked No. 10 Dossier Reveals Al-Qa'ida's British Recruits", *Sunday Times* http://www.timesonline.co.uk/article/0,,2087-1688261,00.html.

[49] James Sturcke, "Intelligence 'Warned of Iraq Terror Link'", *Guardian Unlimited*, July 19, 2005. http://politics.guardian.co.uk/terrorism/story/0,15935,1531732,00.html.

[50] Ibid.

[51] Adequately, this conclusion appears under the paragraph heading "What is the Problem?" See *Report of the Defense Science Board Task Force on Strategic Communication* http://www.acq.osd.mil/dsb/reports/2004-09-Strategic_Communication.pdf.

by Islamic extremism. Donald Rumsfeld draws a clear analogy when he remarked that:

> Today, some think that World War II and the Cold War were black-and-white affairs: good versus evil. But there were always those who thought that we should retreat within our borders . . . Those who warned against the rise of Nazism, fascism and communism were often ridiculed and ignored. The enemy we face today is different from the enemies we have faced in the past, but its goal is similar: to impose its fanatical ideology of hatred on the rest of the world.[52]

President Bush not only rebuked his critics who called for a withdrawal from Iraq, but he also stated that the terrorist threat is "a global force that is the successor to Nazis, communists and fascists of the 20th century";[53] he then made the connection explicit when he expressed that "this nation is at war with Islamic fascists".[54] Bush has also referred to this in a number of different formulae, "Islamo-fascism", "Islamo-fascists", and "Islamic fascism".[55] It is worth noting that this phraseology has become a buzzword among the Republicans at a time when polls show that Americans want US troops to leave Iraq within a year and increasingly, more Americans believe that the invasion of Iraq was a mistake (a recent Zogby poll showed that 42 percent of Americans believe that Bush should be impeached if it was found that he did not tell the truth about his reasons for going to war with Iraq[56]). By associating "Islamo-fascism" with Iraq, which is at the heart of the "war on

[52] Cf., "Progress in the Preparation for the Unthinkable", Office of Homeland Security, Texas A&M University System Health Science Center, www.tamhsc.edu/homeland/

[53] Ibid.

[54] "Bush: U.S. At War With 'Islamic Fascists'", CNN.COM, August 10, 2006 http://www.cnn.com/2006/POLITICS/08/10/washington.terror.plot/index.html.

[55] For an excellent summary of the debates that this word conjured up, see Tom Regan, "Experts, Pundits Debate Use of 'Islamo-Fascist'", *Christian Science Monitor*, August 31, 2006 http://www.csmonitor.com/2006/0831/dailyUpdate.html. For a Muslim analysis of the term, see Enver Masud, "Islamo-Fascism is an Oxymoron", *The Wisdom Fund*, August 31, 2006 http://www.twf.org/News/Y2005/1025-Oxymorons.html and for a useful background to the term "fascism", and its implications as used by President Bush, see Paul R. Dunn, "Islamic Fascism: The Propaganda of Our Times", *The Wisdom Fund*, September 6, 2006, http://www.twf.org/News/Y2006/0906-Fascism.html.

[56] For the "facts" to the build up to the invasion of Iraq, see Laura Miller, "War is Sell", PR Watch.org, http://www.prwatch.org/prwissues/2002Q4/war.html.

terror" (or war on Islamo-fascism), the administration has made it clear that pulling out of Iraq will only heighten this totalitarian threat to the rest of civilization. Jim Lobe notes that the right wing press have increasingly framed the occupation of Iraq and the associated challenges faced by Washington "in the context of the rise of fascism and Nazism in the 1930s", and have consistently outdone other media outlets in using the terms "appeasement", "Hitler", "Iraq" and "Islamofascist".[57]

Introduced by the political elite, promoted by the right wing press, the idea itself is about to find itself shrink-wrapped for mass consumption. The week of October 22–26, 2007 has been declared "Islamo-Fascism Awareness Week"[58] in which two hundred university and college campuses will receive "wake-up calls" to "lies" of the political left that also feature a number of items to educate students on Islamo-Fascism. The "Student's Guide to Hosting Islamo-Fascism Awareness Week" details the essential features of the week, which include the distribution of pamphlets on "The Oppression of Women in Islam", "The Islamic Mein Kampf", "Why Israel is the Victim", a showing of a selection of documentaries (Suicide Killers, Obsession, Islam: What the West Needs to Know or the ABC mini-series, The Path to 9/11) and a "memorial service for the victims of Islamo-Fascist violence around the world". While Bush, when using this term, has made some point that "Islamo-fascism" is not Islam, it is extremely telling that this "Islamo-Fascism Awareness Week" blurs the line between the faith and its perversion by including attacks on the faith with such pamphlets as "the oppression of women *in Islam*". This blurring was actually called into question when Newt Gingrich (*Time* magazine "Man of the Year" and former Republican Speaker of the House of Representatives) argued that while Bush's policies are correct, they failed because they did not "define the scale of the emerging World War III, between the West and the forces of Islam".[59]

The grievous mistake of formulating policy in such a way is that it creates a self-perpetuating cycle—the outcomes of such policies fuel the causes of extremism and terrorism, which in turn actually fuel its thesis.

[57] Jim Lobe, "Fascists? Look Who's Talking", *Asia Times Online*, September 2, 2006, http://www.atimes.com/atimes/Middle_East/HI02Ak04.html.

[58] See http://media1.terrorismawareness.org/files/Islamo-Fascmism-Awareness-Week-Guide.html.

[59] Jim Lobe, "Neo-Con favourite declares WW III", *Asia Times Online*, September 14, 2006, http://www.atimes.com/atimes/Front_Page/HI14Aa02.html.

In trying to understand why Muslims condemned terrorism, most of the respondents to a Gallup world poll cited religious and humanitarian reasons, whereas those that condoned the acts of 9/11 cited secular reasons, namely "occupation and US domination". As the report makes plain, "The real difference between those who condone terrorist acts and all others is politics, not piety". The cold war paradigm was rooted in communism's rejection of Western values and modernity itself, and despite "intense political anger at some Western powers, Muslims do not reject Western values wholesale". Indeed, the report uncovered respondents "admiration for Western technology and democratic values such as freedom of the press and government accountability".[60] Another poll conducted by Terror Free Tomorrow of twenty Muslim countries over the past two years revealed that even those minority Muslims that supported terror attacks by Osama bin Laden and al-Qa'ida actually "approved of specific American actions in their own countries". The findings make clear that "for most people, their professed support of terrorism/bin Laden can be more accurately characterized as a kind of 'protest vote' against current US foreign policies, not as a deeply held religious conviction or even an inherently anti-American or anti-Western view".[61]

Following 9/11, America enjoyed unprecedented good-will from around the world, yet the administration failed to capitalise on it and instead embarked upon a series of misguided policies that have ignored moral and ethical parameters, violated international law, and nurtured an economy on the mass production of weapons.[62] According to many experts, al-Qa'ida is stronger than ever before. The number of terrorist attacks increased by 25 percent in 2006, almost all in Iraq and Afghanistan, claiming more than 20,000 lives. Likewise, many analysts also see the invasions of Iraq and Afghanistan serving as "a major recruiting tool for Islamic militants. The effect [...] has been growing support for Al-Qaeda and similar groups across the Islamic world and in Europe, where millions of

[60] Dalia Mogahed, "Framing the War on Terror", Gallup World Poll, September 11 2007, http://www.gallupworldpoll.com/content/?ci=28678

[61] Kenneth Ballen, "The Myth of Muslim Support for Terror", *Christian Science Monitor*, February 23, 2007 http://www.csmonitor.com/2007/0223/p09s01-coop.html.

[62] Zaid Shakir, "Reflections on 9/11 and Islam", New Islamic Directions Blog, http://www.newislamicdirections.com/nid/notes/reflections_on_9_11_and_ramadan_1/.

Muslims live".[63] With the invasion and occupation of Afghanistan and Iraq, and the continuing threat of expanding military operations to Iran, there is a very real fear that under the guise of fighting extremism, the West is plunging itself into a wider war with the Islamic world. While radical Islam presents a clear challenge to Muslims, they are also deeply disturbed by the continued demonisation of their faith.[64]

MUSLIM INTELLECTUAL RESPONSES TO THE WEST

To comprehend the roots of the ideological expressions of Islam that have been discussed, we must first understand the historical and political context that shaped Muslim attitudes to and perception of the modern world, and to do that, we must understand how Muslim intellectuals first sought to respond to the gradual colonisation of Muslim lands. By the sixteenth and seventeenth centuries, much of the Islamic world was colonised, but it was not until the invasion of Egypt by Napoleon in 1798 that Muslims realised that something was going dreadfully wrong. This reality led to three types of responses by Muslim intellectuals: the puritan-literal, the modernist-reformist and the millenialist. The puritans saw that there was a need to return to the purity of the Qur'ān and the practice of the Prophet Muhammad ﷺ. Not only were they hostile towards modernity, but their wrath was also focused upon other Muslims who they deemed to have fallen into polytheism (*shirk*) by introducing evil innovations that contaminated Islam and weakened Muslims.

The second category of intellectuals varied considerably. While also believing that a return to the pious early generation of Muslims (*salaf*) was necessary, they believed that Islam had to be modernised in order to survive the attack by the West. They concluded that the sources that made the West powerful had to be studied and emulated; namely technology, science and education. Reason was given a much more central position as these Muslim intellectuals tried to synthesise European philosophical thought

[63] Jeffery Donovan, "Terrorism: Six Years On, How Is War Against Al-Qaeda Progressing?" http://www.rferl.org/featuresarticle/2007/9/50BAEF11-ADEF-4E44-A63C-5105217E0D6A.html.

[64] Speaking at the annual Islamic Society of North America (ISNA) convention, Rabbi Eric Yoffie, head of the Union for Reform Judaism, the largest Jewish movement in the United States, conceded that, "… there is no shortage of voices prepared to tell us that fanaticism and intolerance are fundamental to Islamic religion, and that violence and even suicide bombing have deep Quranic roots".

with an "updated" and modern understanding of Islam. Amongst this intelligentsia, diverse calls emerged, including a call to nationalism, for a return to the caliphate and for the restructure of Muslim seminaries along the lines of the European educational system. Others were more drawn to rationalise aspects of Islamic doctrine.

The final reaction to Western domination was by the millenialists, who asserted that oppression would end with the coming of the Mahdi, who would appear prior to the Christ ﷺ towards the end of the world. The battle for independence using these varied responses continued across the Islamic world up to the Second World War, when most Muslim countries achieved independence.[65]

Following the end of the Second World War, a new generation of Muslim intellectuals realised that by embracing western technology, science and education, they had also imported western values and culture. These values were seen as sources of corruption and pollution of Muslim society. These intellectuals sought to fend off the cultural, economic and social domination of their former colonial masters. After the two World Wars, many modernist Muslim ideologues were drawn to Marxist and socialist parties, which were seen as credible alternatives to western liberalism and capitalism, and were initially seen as necessary steps to emancipate the Muslim world from its backwardness. The influence of Marxism over these intellectuals is clearly visible. Through their interpretation of Islam, Islam came to be seen as an "ideology" that brought "radical" changes to society. Muslims now sought a "revolution" to reinstate an Islamic "state". Muslims committed to bringing about this revolution were formed along well-organised and well-disciplined groups. Each group had a leader, agents and "troops". Terminologies alien to the Islamic tradition were introduced, as once again philosophical and ideological trends that were popular in the West were taken up by Muslims. Jihad was seen through the lens of an "anti-imperialist struggle" to resist capitalism that had corrupted humanity. The most violent and radical of these revivalist trends viewed any Muslim that

[65] To understand how Muslim responses to imperialism and colonialism varied from South Asia, Africa, the Ottoman Empire, the Middle East and Egypt, see the classic by Nikki Keddie, *An Islamic Response to Imperialism* (University of California Press, 1983); P.M. Holt, *The Mahdist State in the Sudan* (Oxford: Oxford University Press, 1979); Ayesha Jalal, *Self and Sovereignty: Individual and Community in South Asian Islam since 1850* (London: Routledge, 2000); and Hasan Kayali, *Arabs and Young Turks: Ottomanism, Arabism and Islamism* (University of California Press, 1997).

did not rule by God's law as apostates. Since there was no true Islamic government in the world, these revivalists condemned the entire Muslim world and the "infidel" West. The whole world was now seen as "the abode of war" and jihad was understood to be a state of perpetual war.[66] Only a select few amongst the Muslims were chosen to form a "vanguard" of true believers, whose divine task was to cleanse the world of idolatrous materialism.[67]

The idea of a vanguard is so alien to the Islamic tradition that it more resembles "a concept imported from Europe, through a lineage that stretches back to the Jacobins, through the Bolsheviks and latter-day Marxist guerrillas such as the Baader-Meinhof gang".[68] The current model for radical Islam has not been derived so much from the Qur'ān and the hadīths as from the inspiration drawn from "thinkers such as Nietzsche, Kierkegaard and Heidegger".[69] Indeed, as Olivier Roy observes, "[r]adical Islam is part of and heir of the modern Third Worldist anti-US movement".[70] Roy notes that attacks by radical Muslims today are reminiscent of the "Russian Socialist revolutionaries of the end of the nineteenth century, and the idea that a spectacular attack at the heart of the power will suddenly show the alienated masses that their time has come and they will rise up".[71] The irony is that while showing their intense hatred for the West, al-Qa'ida and those individuals that have any sympathy with them are actually following an Islam that is fused with

[66] See Zaid Shakir, "Jihad as Perpetual War" in Aftab A. Malik ed., *The Empire and the Crescent: Global Implications for a New American Century* (Bristol: Amal Press, 2003) for an examination of this thesis in light of traditional Islamic scholarship.

[67] What I have attempted to capture here are the dominant features of the radical-revivalist strand whose ideology is carried today by groups like al-Qa'ida. For further details on the Arab responses to the challenge of Western powers, see Elie Kedourie, *Afghani and 'Abduh: An Essay on Religious Unbelief and Political Activism in Modern Islam* (London: Frank Cass, 1997). Also see Ibrahim M. Abu-Rabi, *The Intellectual Origins of Islamic Resurgence in the Modern Arab World* (New York: State University of New York Press, 1995); Martin S. Kramer, *Arab Awakening & Islamic Revival: The Politics of Ideas in the Middle East* (New Brunswick, NJ: Transaction Publishers, 1996); John L., Esposito, ed., *Political Islam: Revolution, Radicalism or Reform?* (Boulder, CO: Lynne Rienner Publishers Inc., 1997); Ahmad S. Moussalli, *Moderate and Radical Islamic Fundamentalism: The Quest for Modernity, Legitimacy and the Islamic State* (Gainesville, FL: University Press of Florida, 1999); and David Sagiv, *Fundamentalism and Intellectuals in Egypt, 1973–1993* (London: Frank Cass, 1995).

[68] John Gray, "How Marx turned Muslim", *Independent*, 27 July 2002. http://www.themodernreligion.com/pol/marx-muslim.html.

[69] Ibid.

[70] Olivier Roy, *Globalised Islam. The Search for a New Ummah* (London: Hurst, 2004) p. 50.

[71] Ibid., p. 57.

"Islamicised" nineteenth-century European revolutionary writings.[72] The results of merging a warped interpretation of Islam with ideas that demand blood sacrifice, revolution and anarchy, would have "horrified Muslims in the past".[73]

THE STATE WE ARE IN

Rather than bringing clarity or an intellectual and spiritual awakening, the movements that arose in the Muslim heartlands responded to foreign domination by systematically attacking and undermining past scholarship and spiritual and intellectual leadership. Far from being rooted in traditional Islam, these reformers dismissed it and interpreted Islam in light of the prevailing ideas of the day and as a consequence, Muslims around the world have inherited a legacy of intellectual and spiritual confusion. Today, reform is seen as a key to purging extremism, but it is precisely through reform that extremist groups such as al-Qa'ida are able to construct their jihadist worldview and claim legitimacy. In addition, the extremists and reformers of today share some commonalities.[74] Both want the right to reinterpret Islam as they see fit, and this can only be achieved by dismissing the Islamic tradition. By doing so, both vest every Muslim with the competence to be a jurist. At the heart of both the extremist and the reformist understanding of Islam is the individual: there

[72] See Ian Buruma and Avishai Margalit, *Occidentalism: A Short History of Anti-Westernism* (London: Atlantic Books, 2005). Particularly interesting is the discussion of the "cult of death" (pp. 50–69.), whereby the authors discuss modern day suicide missions of radical Muslims as having historical precedents in "German-style ethnic nationalism—including pan-Germanism". The authors note that "the idea that freelance terrorists would enter paradise as martyrs by murdering unarmed civilians is a modern invention, one that would have horrified Muslims in the past [...]" (p. 69).

[73] Ibid., p. 69. For further discussions in this regard, see John Gray, *Al-Qaeda and What it Means to be Modern* (London: Faber and Faber, 2005) and Roger Scruton, *The West and the Rest: Globalization and the Terrorist Threat* (London: Continuum, 2003).

[74] Note that both the extremist interpretation of Islam and the calls for reform arise out of a sense of injustice. As discussed, the reformist movement originally arose as a response to the challenge/threat by the West. Today, al-Qa'ida and those who share its vision cite US foreign policy and the support for Israel as the cause of the ills of the Muslim world. Reform is argued not only to combat extremism, but for perceived injustices that stem from an outdated sharia law. In the articles that discuss the need for reform, women's rights are almost always cited as having been violated. We should realise that there are truths to all of these grievances: the role of foreign policy in contributing to human suffering *and* Muslim denial that women have had to endure incredible injustices (see notes 79 and 80). The solution to both these crimes is neither extremism nor reform; rather, it is to reassert the Islamic tradition.

is no need to study the traditional Islamic sciences nor is their any need for recourse to the learned scholars, as these give way to an "expression of a personal relationship [...] to faith and knowledge".[75] It should come as no surprise then, to learn that "few al-Qa'ida operatives [...] have a religious education, [with] most having been trained within secular institutions and in technical fields",[76] and it is extremely telling that Osama bin Laden referred to the 9/11 hijackers as belonging to no traditional school of Islamic law.[77] Caught between the terrorists' own reformed and warped version of Islam and cries from the West for an Islamic reformation, the Islamic tradition must be allowed to speak for itself, lest we all face more bloodshed, confusion and misery.

THE ISLAMIC TRADITION

While reference has been made to the term throughout this chapter, it would be wise to clarify what I mean when speaking of "tradition" and "traditional" Islam. This word means many things to different people in various contexts. Often we hear that "tradition" is backward and needs to change and adapt to the times in which we live.[78] Many times when people refer to "tradition" in relation to Islam, they are actually referring to village customs, cultural norms and tribal practices that often *clash* with Islam.[79] At other times, "tradition" is invoked to describe harsh conditions imposed on the weakest members of society by the actions of a section of the Muslim community who adhere to only a part of Islam's legal

[75] Olivier Roy, *Globalised Islam*, p. 28.

[76] Faisal Devji, *Landscapes of the Jihad: Militancy, Morality, Modernity* (London: C. Hurst & Co., 2005) p. xiii.

[77] His exacts words were "Those youths who conducted the operations did not accept any *fiqh* (school of Islamic law) in the popular terms [...]". Cf., Ibid., p. 13. (Osama bin Laden's words are taken from a transcript translated by George Michael and Kassem M. Wahba referenced in the book.)

[78] See Nazim Baksh, *In the Spirit of Tradition* http://masud.co.uk/ISLAM/misc/misc.htm for an interesting discussion along this theme.

[79] While Islam was not sent to erase culture or local practices (Imam Mālik included local custom as an essential part of his legal principles), these practices are examined in light of the sharia. If they are not found to contradict its principles, then that custom or practice continues. Today, much of the harm that "traditional" Islam is accused of is actually the result of those perpetuating acts of aggression. Practices that have no place in Islam (usually carried out against women and children) are often cited by the media *and by the aggressors* as being sanctioned by Islam. These practices include forced arranged marriages, honour killings, sexual assault, domestic violence and the prevention of education.

tradition. In doing so, they pursue the letter of the law rather than the spirit of the law and neglect other aspects of the Islamic tradition.[80]

In this discussion, "tradition" is invoked in the context of an inherited scholastic methodology and set of paradigms. Included are the debates; the dissenting opinions; and the scholarly exegesis, interpretation and understanding of the ethical, moral, legal, spiritual and philosophical traditions of Islam. Therefore, "tradition" in this sense refers to a transmission: a handing down of something. Those who transmit this tradition have deep roots in scholarship. This scholarship is bound together by a tapestry of interconnecting chains of transmissions of other scholars, mystics, philosophers, jurists, theologians and sages that reach back generations,[81] leading ultimately to the Prophet Muhammad ﷺ wherein its authority is confirmed. Central to this authority is mercy, as the first tradition of the Prophet Muhammad ﷺ that is taught by the teacher to the student, is: "The merciful are shown mercy by the Merciful one. Show mercy to those on earth and you will be shown mercy by the One in Heaven". From this central tenant of the Islamic tradition, Muslim scholars have understood that in every matter, Muslims should be just, merciful and wise—anything that is lacking in any one of these principles cannot be said to be derived from sacred law. What keeps the tradition living and dynamic is the scholar who is trained to understand

[80] Often, the victims of these fatwas are women. It would be of interest to examine the way in which imams are trained to understand, interpret and apply the sharia in the modern world. It would also be interesting to see the level of education that the average imam has *prior* to joining a madrasa, or seminary and to compare modern requirements with those stipulated in the past. In the sixteenth century, an advertisement was placed for the position of Imam of the Grand Mosque in Istanbul. There were seven requirements that any potential applicant had to meet before they could apply: 1) To have mastered the languages of Arabic, Latin, Turkish and Persian; 2) To have mastered the Qur'ān, the Bible and the Torah; 3) To be a scholar in sharia and *fiqh*; 4) To have mastered physics and mathematics up to teaching standard; 5) To be a master of chivalry, archery, duelling and the arts of jihad; 6) To be of handsome countenance; and 7) To have a strong melodious voice. Cf., *Emel: The Muslim Lifestyle Magazine* 13 (October 2005), p. 41. One wonders how many imams today could match or exceed these sixteenth-century expectations.

[81] This chain is normally referred to as an *isnād*, which is linked to the system of *ijazah* (licence to teach), which is conveyed upon an individual who has reached a degree of mastery over a particular discipline or text, which they themselves can then authorise others to teach. It carried with it authority, since it was only given by masters who themselves had received it from their teachers and so on until this chain reached back to first generation of Muslims (*al-salaf*) and to the Prophet Muhammad ﷺ himself. Now the importance of having an isnād, and a system for its controlled perpetuation, the ijazah, is belittled and its significance ignored by the emergence of an increasing auto-didacticism. As a consequence, authoritative Islamic rulings have been substituted for the authoritarian opinions of those who possess little or no traditional Islamic education. The results have been shown to be disastrous.

both the tradition *and* the modern world in which they live and to which the sacred is applied.[82]

TAJDĪD: THE PROCESS OF RENEWAL

If America and Britain need to rethink and reassess their foreign policies, mainstream Muslims also face critical choices and challenges. The existence of individuals with misguided enthusiasm in Islam should hardly be surprising. All religious traditions have suffered from this dilemma at one time or another and Islam, sadly, is no exception. Traditional Islam, the normative voice of Islam throughout the centuries, must be empowered to reclaim the discourse of hatred from individuals. While there may be some scepticism about the usefulness of learning any lessons from ex-Islamists,[83] the inescapable fact that is reinforced is the need for traditional Islamic jurisprudence and theology to counter this odious, indiscriminate theology that animates hatred. What the Muslim world requires is a process of *tajdīd*, or "renewal". The core traditional Islamic values of mercy, compassion, peace and beauty, those that honour the sanctity of all life have been swept aside in a politically charged Muslim world and they urgently need to be re-established. Muslims need to renew their ethical and moral commitments that are so clearly enumerated in the Qur'ān and embodied in the practice of the Prophet Muhammad ﷺ. Our scholars have explained that the process of tajdīd includes reviving the hearts of people, spreading justice, upholding fairness and avoiding the shedding of blood.

The spread of knowledge is therefore the first necessary step to infuse Muslims with vitality and dynamism, and for this to begin, the scholars must play a leading role. There needs to be a comprehensive programme of training, education and learning at all levels of the Muslim community. Women must also play an essential role in this renewal and can no longer

[82] A clear example of the application of traditional Islamic legal philosophy in the modern context is Shaykh Afifi's fatwa in this collection. It would be well noted that while there are many well-argued explanations for 9/11 and 7/7, mostly vis-à-vis foreign policies, nonetheless, those who planned, executed and supported it could not have justified it, had they been trained in this traditional educational model that the first generation of Muslims articulated, developed and lived by.

[83] See: Ali Eteraz, "Media Reliance on Former Terrorists and Radicals is a Joke", *Huffington Post*, July 3 2007, http://www.huffingtonpost.com/ali-eteraz/media-reliance-on-former-_b_54842.html.

be left behind, forgotten or ignored. The Muslim community also needs leadership that is rooted in traditional learning, encapsulated in a moral and ethical outlook. Myopia has robbed our intellectual discourse of any coherent vision for too long. As a result, there is an emerging community of young Muslims in Britain that believe any means is justified to achieve their political ends. This is a huge departure from normative Islam, which values prudence and courage, not zealotry; temperance and justice rather than hate. Zealotry and hate are specific traits identified as detrimental to the soul and Islam's spiritual tradition has always played a vital role in purging these diseases from the heart. In the contemporary world however, these diseases have been invaluable in recruiting and nurturing a subculture of Muslims that view unfolding events behind a lens of conspiracy theories, theological neuroses and religious illiteracy. A deadly cocktail if ever there was one.

If it can be said that some non-Muslims suffer from ignorance about Islam, then it must be added that there are numerous Muslims who are ignorant about their own tradition. Expressed as an ideology anchored in opposition to the West, and determined to wage a universal jihad, these Muslims reduce Islam to a violent anti-intellectual force. Even when retaliating against transgressions by an enemy, the classical Islamic jurists not only understood that acts of terrorism were punishable by death, but they viewed these acts as cowardly and even contrary to the ethics of Arab chivalry. Muslims today must be strong and frank. We need to *support justice* even if it is against ourselves, as the Qur'ān instructs. Islam teaches that with affliction comes the strengthening of belief, not its corruption. When faced by threat and persecution, Muslims turn to the prayer of Prophets: "God is enough for us—and what an excellent Guardian!" This is how faith is articulated when we have trust in God at all times. When faith is replaced by tribalism, the response is different; Muslims experience the states of hopelessness, blame, resentment and helplessness. Prayer is substituted for rhetoric and rhetoric leads to hate. In this state, Islam has been enmeshed by the emotions of anger, hate and revenge; emotions which Islam views as detrimental to the human soul.

3 Shared Values

'ABDALLAH BIN BAYYAH

THE STUDY OF values comes under the broader field of ethics, the field of enquiry that looks into what is good and correct with respect to standards that may be personal or cultural, and can be used as a normative standard for behaviour. Values can be defined as ethical principles that determine honourable and praiseworthy conduct, where acting contrarily is shameful and worthy of condemnation.

Philosophers have debated since time immemorial about whether there are such things as universal values. There is agreement that shared values exist on a cultural level. Specific societies all have norms and values that are derived from custom, tradition, or religious belief. The dispute is whether there are any values that transcend the confines of a particular society or culture and are shared by all of humanity.

The dispute hinges on the question of the true nature of values. Is there an absolute and objective standard of what is good? Is "good" something universal? Or is it always relative and subjective, dependent on the interests of an individual or group? This is a point of fierce philosophical debate that has engendered numerous schools of ethical thought, including utilitarianism, pragmatism, and idealism, as well as a host of applications for economics, politics, and political science. I will not dwell on each of these schools of thought on its own. Rather, I will discuss two general philosophical tendencies, that of moral relativism and that of universalism. Then I will discuss what Islam teaches about this matter.

Moral relativists believe that there are no universal values and that moral or ethical propositions do not reflect absolute and universal moral truths; relativists instead make claims relative to social and cultural circumstances that vary according to time and place. Conditions for people living in the Arabian desert are different than those for people living in a valley in the Himalayas, or on the Chinese coast, or the Indian coast, or along a great river delta. Then—the relativists argue—there is the obscurity and capriciousness of how moral standards are conceptually understood. There are various concepts of property, family, marriage, reason, and of God. Norms of conduct that prevail over one environment in a given historical era could very well be destructive if transplanted to another. Each society faces specific challenges at various times in its history. The ideal solutions to these challenges will necessarily differ.

Consequently—the relativists argue—the idea that there are universal normative truths that are suitable for guiding the lives of all people at all times is simply absurd.

Moral universalists hold the opposite view, that there is a single and timeless ethical standard. Some system of ethics applies universally to all people regardless of culture, environment, or historical era. The same standards hold true for someone in China, Spain, or Paraguay. They were the same for the people of Ancient Greece and Medieval Europe as they are for us living today and as they will continue to be for all times. What was evil in the past will remain evil in the future. Moral laws do not change with the times. Ethical standards are neither "Eastern" nor Western".

The idea of moral universalism can be traced back to the revealed religions, especially those religions which claim to have a universal message. The philosopher Hunter Mead expresses this idea in the context of Western Christianity, explaining that the idea that there is a single deity who governs the affairs of the world which He created is the basis for Western religious thinking. This idea has also been defended on the basis of logic. This approach was taken by Kant, who may well be the most famous of all philosophers of ethics. He believed that analysis can consistently demonstrate that the violation of moral law is simultaneously the violation of logic. Anti-ethical behaviour is always contradictory.

One of the examples that Kant gives to illustrate this point is making a promise. When a person makes a promise that he has no intention of fulfilling, his behaviour is morally wrong. This is because his behaviour is based simultaneously upon two contradictory principles. The first of these principles is that people should believe promises. The fact that I have broken my promise expresses another principle—that an individual has the right to break his promise. This is the case as long as we accept that moral law applies to everyone. However, if every person who makes a promise breaks it, then no one would believe a promise. This results in a principle that no one should believe promises, which is directly contradictory to our first principle.

THE ISLAMIC PERSPECTIVE

As Muslims, our intellectual outlook supports the existence of shared values. The basis for this belief is as follows:

1. Islam establishes the idea of absolute equality between all human beings and that they are descended from a common ancestor. They have one Lord and they share one father. Allah says: *O humankind! We have indeed created you from a man and a woman and made you into nations and tribes to know one another.* (Qur'ān 49: 13)

   The Prophet Muhammad ﷺ said: "O humankind! Your Lord is one Lord, and you have one father. All of you are from Adam, and Adam is from dust. The noblest of you is the most God-fearing. No Arab has and superiority over a non-Arab, no non-Arab has any superiority over an Arab, no black person has any superiority over a white person, and no white person has any superiority over a black person—superiority is only through piety".[1]

2. Islam asserts that all human beings are created with a natural inclination towards goodness, towards, truth, and towards faith in Allah. Allah says: *So set thy purpose* [O Muhammad] *for religion as a man by nature upright—the nature* [framed] *of Allah, in which He hath created the human being. There is no altering* [the laws of] *Allah's creation.* (Qur'ān 30: 30)

[1] Sunan al-Tirmidhī.

No matter how protracted and never-ending the debate might be among philosophers whether moral values are universal or relative, common sense tells us that shared values do exist. The best proofs for this are the human faculties of reason (which Descartes considered the greatest thing distributed among humanity) and of language. Every rational mind recognises justice and every language has a word for it—a word which is recognised as having a positive and noble meaning. The same can be said for "truth", "liberty", "tolerance", "integrity" and many other concepts. These are praised by all cultures and expressed positively in all languages.

The opposites of these concepts are regarded with derision and rejected, like "tyranny" and "oppression". If we were to address the most despotic person as a "tyrant", he would take offence. He would prefer to be described as just. Likewise, even a liar dislikes to be named as such. "Deception" and "bigotry" are likewise words that people have an aversion to, regardless of what cultural background they have. Is this not evidence for the existence of shared values? These shared values need to be actively promoted in the world today, and not just the essential human rights that are indispensable for human beings to be able to live with each other. Rather, these shared values are much more embracing, like mercy, kindness, and the generosity to help those who are in need regardless of their race, religion, or country of origin. We need to incorporate these values into our understanding of human relations, so that we will not only uphold the principle of human equality in a neutral way, but embrace the "other" with warmth, love, and a true sense of brotherhood. An old Arab saying—which is found in one form or another in all languages—goes: "Treat others the way that you wish to be treated".

The Prophet Muhammad ﷺ once said: "No one truly believes until he wants for his brother what he wants for himself".[2] The value of "human brotherhood" is being joined with that of "love" in these words of our Prophet ﷺ. Before somebody accuses me of reinterpreting this *ḥadīth* for my own purposes, they should know that this is the understanding of the scholars from centuries back. For instance, the leading Ḥanbalī jurist, Ibn Rajab (d.1392CE/795 AH) said: "The brotherhood referred to in this ḥadīth

[2] As related in the *Saḥiḥ* of al-Bukhārī and elsewhere.

is the brotherhood of humanity".[3] The same is asserted by al-Shabrakhītī (d. 1694 CE /1106 AH) and many others.

Love is an essential value, since all people desire to be loved. It is extremely rare to find a person who desires to be despised by others. When love is realised by both parties, hostilities come to an end. Love is an emotional state as well as a mode of conduct. The Prophet Muhammad ﷺ encouraged us to proclaim our love, saying: "If one of you loves his brother, he should let him know it".[4] Love is a shared value, since all people are pleased with it, even those who do not act according to its dictates. This is the true test for a shared value—that everyone wishes to be regarded as possessing it. No one wants to be described as "unjust" or "intolerant". Such values, in spite of their universality, can wilt and become dormant if they are not nurtured and encouraged. An Arab poet once wrote:

> "These noble values grow like flowering plants/When they are watered from a noble spring".

One of the most important values that can solve the world's problems is that of respecting diversity, indeed loving it—regarding it as a source of enrichment and beauty, as an essential element of the human experience. When we navigate our differences successfully and aspire to conduct ourselves in a most noble manner above and beyond the legislation of human rights, then we establish a basis for applying our shared values to bring harmony from our differences and to bring love in place of enmity.

Allah tells us in the Qur'ān: *Repel evil with what is best, and then the one between whom and you had been enmity will become as your dearest friend.* (41: 34) The message of this verse is that goodness brings about goodness and love engenders love. Can we not then hope to foster these shared human values by making our own conduct exemplary—by being tolerant, generous, honest, and trustworthy and thereby convincing the "other" who is just as human and who shares the same love for these values? Good conduct results in reciprocal good conduct. Generosity cultivates generosity. Convincing others of the ways of goodness is the

[3] Al-Nawawī, *Sharḥ al-'Arba'īn* 123. Editor's note: for a further commentary on this particular ḥadīth, refer to the explanation by Shaykh Muhammad Afifi available at: http://mac.abc.se/home/onesr/d/mubn_e.pdf

[4] Al-Bukhārī, *Adab al-Mufrad.*

most important humanitarian issue. We wish to take from Plato his words when he said: "The morality of the world is an expression of the victory of the power to convince over the power of force".

The values of humanity lie in their ability to have conviction—to convince and to be convinced by various means of substituting one thing for another. There are things which are better and others which are worse. Civilization is essentially the preservation of a mode of life by means of the inherent conviction to respond by choosing what is best. The use of force, under any circumstances, is a failure of civilization, regardless of whether we are talking about society in general or the individual.

The harmony that we must aspire to is not just between various cultures and societies. We must bring about such harmony within the individual as well. People have a varied cultural heritage, which sometimes develops into a crisis of values within the individual, and which needs to be transformed into inner harmony and a source of personal enrichment. A person can be of Asian origin, Muslim by faith, and British by nationality and upbringing—all at the same time.

By cultivating the value of tolerance over violence and hate, we channel people's energies into productive activity that contributes to the general welfare. No one should ever resort to warfare or to violence to further their goals.

Religious leaders need to do their part to promote these universal values. They should be part of the solution and not part of the problem, as we have unfortunately found to be the case for certain representatives of all faiths. Religious leaders should not stir up tensions in a hope to gain the approval of their followers at the expense of human solidarity and mutual understanding. Likewise, the media, the universities, and civic organisations have their roles to play in fostering these shared human values. Political leaders also should do their part. They should find ways to alleviate poverty and oppression whenever they are found. They should look for solutions to the issues of our time, even if they can only achieve partial solutions and partial justice. Military means to solve these problems are unethical and they do not work.

To conclude, I wish to draw attention to three objectives that we, as Muslim scholars, need to focus on. We need to:

1. Present convincing lessons on these values to the people of the West, specifically to the Muslims living there, that will prevent them from ever committing acts of violence or terror.

2. Address the responsible agencies in the West to assure the Muslims their cultural rights, so that they can be a positive element in society whose particular identity does not contradict with European society in any essential way.

3. Invite the people of the West to take another look at their relations with the Muslim world in light of these values so that together we establish a world in which we all coexist to the benefit of us all. This is the way that is most ethical, most intelligent, and most rewarding.

4 | Tribulation, Patience and Prayer*

HAMZA YUSUF

Q: The convenient response to those who revile your religion is to return the favour. The more virtuous position however is to forgive. Forgiveness as you know, while less in virtue when compared to love, nevertheless, can result in love. Love, by definition, does not require forgiveness. What many Muslims today seem to forget is that ours is a religion of love and our Prophet ﷺ was the *Ḥabīb*, the Beloved. How did love, the defining virtue of our community, come to be replaced by an urge to redress wrongs, to punish instead of to forgive?

A: It is the result of Muslims seeing themselves as victims. Victimization is a defeatist mentality. It's the mentality of the powerless. The word victim is from the Latin "victima" which carries with it the idea of the one who suffers injury, loss, or death due to a voluntary undertaking. In other words, "the victim of one's own actions". Muslims never really had a mentality of victimization. From a metaphysical perspective, which is always the first and primary perspective of a Muslim, there can be no victims. We believe that all suffering has a redemptive value.

Q: If the tendency among Muslims is to view themselves as victims, which appears to me as a fall from grace, what virtue must we then

* This interview was conducted by Nazim Baksh, a broadcast correspondent with the Canadian Broadcasting Corporation. Nazim has recently been producing and reporting for news documentaries focusing on the root causes of terrorism and the motivations of those who support or become members of terrorist organisations such as al-Qa'ida.

cultivate to dispense with this mental and physical state that we now find ourselves in?

A: The virtue of patience is missing. Patience is the first virtue after *ṭawba* or repentance. Early Muslim scholars considered patience as the first *maqām* or station in the realm of virtues that a person entered into. Patience in Islam means patience in the midst of adversity. A person should be patient in what has harmed or afflicted him. Patience means that you don't lose your comportment or your composure. If you look at the life of the Prophet Muhammad ﷺ you will never find him losing his composure. Patience was a hallmark of his character. He was "the unperturbed one", which is one of the meanings of *ḥalīm: wa kāna aḥlam an-nās*. He was the most unperturbed of humanity. Nothing fazed him either inwardly or outwardly because he was with God in all his states.

Q: Patience is a beautiful virtue. [I recall] the cry of Prophet Jacob ﷺ: "*fa ṣabran jamīl*" ["So I must observe beautiful patience"[1]]. Patience, it appears, is not an isolated virtue but rather it is connected to a network of virtues. Should Muslims focus on this virtue at the expense of the other virtues?

A: The traditional virtues of a human being were four and Qāḍī ibn al-ᶜArabī considered them to be the foundational virtues, or the *ummahāt ul faḍā'il* of all of humanity. They are: prudence, courage, temperance and justice. Prudence, or rather practical wisdom, and courage, are defining qualities of the Prophet Muhammad ﷺ. He said that God loves courage even in the killing of a harmful snake. Temperance is the ability to control oneself. Incontinence, the hallmark of intemperance, is said to occur when a person is unable to control himself. In modern medicine it is used to refer to someone who can't control his urine or faeces. But not so long ago the word incontinence meant a person who was unable to control his temper, appetite or sexual desire. Temperance is the moral virtue that moderates one's appetite in accordance with prudence. In early

[1] Editor's note: This was said by the Prophet Jacob ﷺ upon receiving false news from his sons that Joseph ﷺ had been eaten by a wolf. He also repeated this years later, when Joseph ﷺ, now a chief official in the Egyptian monarchy, told his brothers (who did not recognise him) that they would not be able to return with their youngest brother, Benjamin, to their father (see Qur'ān 12:18 and 12:83).

Muslim scholarship on Islamic ethics, justice was considered impossible without the virtues of prudence, courage and temperance.

Generosity as a virtue is derived from courage because a generous person is required to be courageous in the face of poverty. Similarly, humility is a derivative from temperance because the humble person will often restrain the urge to brag and be a show-off because he or she sees their talents and achievements as a gift from God and not from themselves. Patience as a virtue is attached to the virtue of courage because the patient person has the courage to endure difficulties. So *ḥilm* (from which you get *ḥalīm*), often translated as forbearance or meekness, is frowned upon in our society. Yet it is the virtue we require to stem the powerful emotion of anger. Unrestrained anger often leads to rage and rage can lead to violence in its various shades.

Our predecessors were known for having an incredible degree of patience while an increasing number of us are marked with an extreme degree of anger, resentment, hate, rancour and rage. These are negative emotions, which present themselves as roadblocks to living a virtuous life.

A patient human being will endure tribulations, trials, difficulties and hardships, if confronted with them. The patient person will not be depressed or distraught and whatever confronts him will certainly not lead to a loss of comportment. God says in the Qur'ān: "*Iṣbirū*". "Have patience and enjoin each other to patience". The beauty of patience is that God is with the patient ones ("*innAllāha ma'aṣ-ṣābirīn*"). God says in the Qur'ān: "*Ista' īnū bi-ṣabiri waṣ-ṣalāt*". *Ista'nā* is a reflexive of the Arabic verb "'*anā*" which is "to help oneself". God is telling us to help ourselves with patience and prayer. This is amazing because the Prophet Muhammad ﷺ said "if you take help, take help from God alone". And so in the Qur'ān, God says: "*Ista' īnū bi-ṣabiri waṣ-ṣalāt*". This means taking help from patience and prayer because that is the means by which God has given you to take help from Him alone. How is it then that a person sees himself as a victim when all calamities, difficulties and trials, are ultimately tests from God. This does not mean the world is free of aggression and that victims have suddenly vanished. What I am talking about is a person's psychology in dealing with hardships.

The sacred law has two perspectives when looking at acts of aggression that are committed by one party against another. When it is viewed by those in authority the imperative is to seek justice. However, from the perspective of the wronged, it is not to seek justice but instead to forgive. Forgiveness, "*ʿafwā*" or to pardon someone is not a quality of authority. A court is not set up to forgive. It's the plaintiff that's required to forgive if there is going to be any forgiveness at all. Forgiveness will not come from the *qāḍī* or the judge. The court is set up to give justice but Islam cautions us not to go there in the first place because "by the standard which you judge so too shall you be judged". That's the point. If you want justice, if you want God, the Supreme Judge of all affairs, to be just to others on your behalf, then you should know that your Lord will use the same standard with you. Nobody on the "Day of Arafat" will pray: "Oh God, be just with me". Instead you will hear them crying: "O God, forgive me, have mercy on me, have compassion on me, overlook my wrongs". Yet, these same people are not willing to forgive, have compassion and mercy on other creatures of God.

Q: Imām al-Ghazālī argued that for these virtues to be effective they had to be in harmony. Otherwise, he said, virtues would quickly degenerate into vices. Do you think that these virtues exist today among Muslims but that they are out of balance? For example, the Arabs in the time of the Prophet ﷺ had courage, but without justice it was bravado. Prudence without justice is merely shrewdness. Do you think that Muslims are clamouring for justice but have subsumed the virtues of temperance and prudence?

A: Yes. Muslims want courage and justice but they don't want temperance and prudence. The four virtues relate to the four humours in the body. Physical sickness is related to spiritual sickness and when these four are out of balance, spiritual and moral sickness occurs. So when courage is the sole virtue, you no longer have prudence. You are acting courageously but imprudently and it's no longer courage but impetuousness. It appears as courage but it is not. A person who is morally incapable of controlling his appetite has incontinence and thus he cannot be prudent nor courageous because part of courage is to constrain oneself when it is appropriate. Imām al-Ghazālī says that courage is a mean between impetuousness and cowardice. The interesting point to note about the four virtues is that you either take them all or you don't take them at all. It's a packaged deal. There is a strong argument among moral ethicists that justice is the result of the first three being in perfect balance.

Q: You have painted a very interesting landscape in terms of Muslim behaviour in the contemporary period but we are seeing evidence of resentment among some Muslims today which is very strange indeed. I am wondering how this might be related to a sense of victimization?

A: There is a very strong correlation. Look for example at the word injury. It comes from *injuria*, a Latin word that means unjust. So if I perceive my condition as unjust it is contrary to the message of the Qur'ān. Whatever circumstances we find ourselves in we hold ourselves as responsible. It gets tricky to navigate especially when it comes to the oppressor and the oppressed. The Prophet Muhammad ﷺ along with the early Muslim community, spent thirteen years purifying themselves in Makkah. These were years of oppression and thus serious self-purification accompanied by an ethic of non-violence, forbearance, meekness and humility. They were then given permission to migrate and to defend themselves. At this point they were not a people out to get vengeance and they were certainly not filled with resentment because they saw everything as coming from God. I'm not talking about being pleased with injustice because that's prohibited. At the same time we accept the world our Lord has put us into and we see everything as being here purposefully, not without purpose, whether we understand it or not. The modern Christian fundamentalists always talk about Islam as a religion devoid of love. It's a very common motif in these religious fundamentalist books that attack Islam. They say "our religion is the religion of love and Islam is the religion of hate, animosity and resentment". Unfortunately, many Muslims have adopted it as their religion, but that doesn't mean resentment has anything to do with Islam.

Love (*maḥaba*) is the highest religious virtue in Islam. Imām al-Ghazālī said that it is the highest *maqām* or spiritual station. It is so because trust, *zuhd* (doing without), fear and hope are stations of this world and so long as you are in this world these stations are relevant, but once you die they can no longer serve you. Love is eternal because love is the reason you were created. You were created to adore God. That's why in Latin the word "adore", which is used for worship in English, is also a word for love, adoration. You were created to worship God, in other words, to love Him because you can't truly adore something or worship something that you don't love. If you are worshipping out of fear, like Imām al-Ghazālī says, it's not the highest level of worship, but the lowest.

Q: A vast number of young Muslims today who have the energy to run down the road of hate do so thinking that it is a display of their faith. What do you say to help them understand that hating wrongs has to be balanced with the virtues of mercy, justice, forgiveness, generosity, etc.

A: The challenge is to get your object of hate right and hate it for the right reason. In other words, there are things that we should hate for the sake of God. Oppression is something that you should hate. It's not *ḥarām* (prohibited) to hate the oppressor, but don't hate them to the degree that it prevents you from being just because that is closer to *taqwā* (awe of God). The higher position is to forgive for the sake of God. God gives you two choices—the high road or the low road—both of them will get you to paradise. We should strive for the highest. Anger is a useful emotion. God created anger in order that we could act and respond to circumstances that need to be changed. Indignation is a beautiful word. Righteous indignation is a good quality and even though it is misused in modern English it's actually a good thing. It means to be angry for the right reasons and then it is to be angry to the right degree because God says, "Do not let the loathing of a people prevent you from being just".

Part 2 THE LAW OF JIHAD

5 Indiscriminate Killing in Light of Islamic Sacred Texts

SUHEIL LAHER

ISLAMIC RULINGS ARE derived from the Qur'ān (the word of God revealed by the angel Gabriel to the Prophet Muhammad ﷺ) and the *sunna* (the way shown by the Prophet, including his sayings, deeds, and tacit approvals or disapprovals). What follows is a compilation of Muslim sacred texts in condemnation of wanton destruction and indiscriminate killing.

FROM THE QUR'ĀN

1. [...] *We decreed upon the Children of Israel that whoever kills a soul—unless for a soul*[1] *or for corruption* [done] *in the land*[2]*—it is as if he had slain mankind entirely. And, whoever saves one, it is as if he had saved mankind entirely*. (Qur'ān, 5:32)

   This verse establishes the sanctity of life.

2. [...] *And do not kill the soul*[3] *which God has forbidden except by right* [...]. (Qur'ān, 6:151)

3. *And do not kill the soul which God has forbidden except by right. And whoever is killed unjustly, We have given his heir authority*[4] *but let him not exceed limits in* [the matter of] *taking life. Indeed, he has been supported* [*by the law*]. (Qur'ān, 17:33)

[1] i.e. in legal retribution for murder, through the requisite channels of justice.

[2] i.e. that requiring the death penalty, again through the requisite legal channels.

[3] i.e. person.

[4] Grounds for legal action.

4. *And* [the believers are] *those who do not invoke any deity with God, nor kill the soul which God has forbidden except by right, nor commit zinā.*[5] (Qur'ān, 25:68)

   This verse conveys the heinousness of unjustifiably taking a human life, and indicates that wrongful murder is close in enormity to *shirk*[6] and *zinā*.

5. *And fight, in the path of God, those who fight you* [...]. (Qur'ān, 2:190)

   This verse indicates that only those involved in combat are to be fought, which *excludes* non-combatants such as women, children and civilians; a regulation detailed further by narrations from the sunna, as mentioned in the following section.

6. *Among mankind is he whose speech impresses you in worldly life, and he calls God to witness as to what is in his heart, yet he is the fiercest of opponents. And, when he goes away, he strives throughout the land to cause corruption therein, and to destroy crops*[7] *and lives.*[8] *And God does not love corruption.* (Qur'ān, 2:204–5)

[5] Illicit sexual intercourse. The Arabic word encompasses both fornication and adultery.

[6] Polytheism or associating partners with God, a sin which is never forgiven to one who dies insistent upon it, as declared in Qur'ān 4:116.

[7] The Arabic word used here, *al-ḥarth*, is generally understood, based on its common lexical meaning, to refer to crops, but see the next footnote for other explanations. *Al-Qāmūs al-Muḥīṭ* also mentions one of the meanings as "earnings".

[8] The Arabic word I have translated here as "lives" is *al-nasl*, which a number of English translations of the Qur'ān have translated as "cattle"—an inaccurate translation as we shall proceed to explain. *Al-Qāmūs al-Muḥīṭ*, an authoritative dictionary of classical Arabic, explains *al-nasl* to be created beings, or offspring. Renowned exegetes have mentioned similar explanations. Qurṭubī says, "*al-nasl* is the child which emanates from any [type of] female". See *Al-Jāmi' li-Ahkām al-Qur'ān*, 3/19. Ālūsī says, "*al-nasl* is every being with a soul [...]. Al-Azharī [an authority in Arabic] said: *al-ḥarth* here is women [as in Qur'ān, 2:223] and *al-nasl* is children. [And it is reported] from [Imām] al-Ṣādiq that *al-ḥarth* here is the religion, and *al-nasl* is people". See *Rūḥ al-Ma'ānī*, 2/144. Shaykh Zādah Rūmī says, in his marginal annotations on Bayḍāwī's exegesis, "*al-nasl* is the noun of *yansilu*, used when something emerges distinct from something else, [...] and so the child is the *nasl* of his parents". See *Ḥāshiyat* Shaykh Zādah *'alā Tafsīr al-Qāḍī al-Bayḍāwī*, 1/514. This selection of quotes establishes clearly that the meaning of *al-nasl* encompasses life in general, and is not restricted to cattle. Perhaps the reason why some translators selected the word cattle here is that the verse, when revealed, first referred to a man at that time named al-Akhnas ibn Shurayq al-Thaqafī, who matched the description of the verses, and destroyed crops and cattle [details of the incident can be perused in most books of Qur'ānic exegesis], which in turn led some briefer exegetes to explain *al-nasl* as cattle. However, there is unanimity among

These verses indicate that wanton destruction and indiscriminate killing are tantamount to working mischief / corruption upon the earth.

FROM THE SUNNA

Prohibition against causing suffering even to animals

1. "A woman entered the Fire on account of a cat, which she tied up, neither feeding it, nor letting it eat [for itself] from the vermin of the earth, until it died, and as a result she entered the Fire [of Hell]".[9]

2. "Do not take something with a soul as a target".[10]

   Another version says, "Ibn 'Umar passed by some youths of Quraysh who had set up a bird and were shooting at it, giving any arrows which missed to the owner of the bird. Thereupon, Ibn 'Umar said, 'God curses the one who does this. Verily, the Messenger of God cursed the one who takes something with a soul as a target'".[11]

   Two variant versions record that, "The Messenger of God forbade taking something with a soul as a target"[12] and that "God curses the one who takes something with a soul as a target".[13]

3. "Indeed, God tortures those who torture people in this world".[14]

scholars—indeed among all rational people—that the import and significance of Qur'ānic verses derives from the general implication of their wording, and is not restricted to the specifics of the circumstances or situation in which they were revealed. See Suyūṭī's *Al-Itqān fī 'Ulūm al-Qur'ān* ("The Perfection in the Sciences of the Qur'ān"), 1/39-40. Hence, there appear no grounds for departing from the literal and general implication of *al-nasl* as "life", and replacing it with "cattle".

[9] Narrated by Bukhārī and Muslim.

[10] Narrated by Muslim, Nasā'ī, Ibn Mājah and Aḥmad.

[11] Narrated by Muslim via Ibn 'Umar as quoted, and by Nasā'ī via two routes (Ibn 'Umar and Ibn 'Abbās) but without mention of the incident of the bird.

[12] Narrated by Tirmidhī (who graded it *ḥasan ṣaḥīḥ*) and Aḥmad, via Ibn 'Abbās. Both of them included mention of Ibn 'Abbās witnessing an incident involving a pigeon, similar to that witnessed by Ibn 'Umar as in the preceding narration.

[13] Narrated by Aḥmad, through a sound, continuous chain of transmitters (Hushaym-Abū Bishr-Sa'īd ibn Jubayr-Ibn 'Umar).

[14] Narrated by Muslim, Abū Dāwūd and Aḥmad.

The narrator of this *ḥadīth*, Ḥakīm ibn Ḥizām, saw some people in the Levant who had had oil poured over their heads and were being made to stand in the hot sun as a punishment for not paying taxes, and he cited the ḥadīth in condemnation of this. This establishes the severe prohibition of inflicting torturous suffering on people, even when they are duly-convicted criminals.

4. "Do not punish with the punishment of God, the Mighty, the Majestic".[15]

   This ḥadīth specifically prohibits the infliction of burning on human beings.

PROHIBITIONS AGAINST WRONGFULLY TAKING LIFE

5. "A Muslim remains in latitude concerning his religion as long as he does not take a life".[16]

6. "Avoid the seven ruinous [sins] […] associating partners with God, sorcery, unlawfully taking life which God has prohibited, consuming interest (*ribā*), consuming the property of an orphan, fleeing on the day of marching [in battle], and accusing a chaste, unaware believing woman of adultery".[17]

SPECIFIC NARRATIONS REGULATING KILLING DURING WAR

7. Ribāḥ ibn al-Rabīʿ al-Tamīmī says, "We were with the Messenger of God in a battle. He saw people gathered, and then he saw a slain woman, whereupon he said, 'This [woman] was not fighting!'"[18]

   Two other versions add, "Thereupon, the Prophet objected to the killing of women and children"[19] and "Catch up with Khālid and

[15] Narrated by Aḥmad (with this wording), as well as by Bukhārī, Tirmidhī (who graded it *ṣaḥīḥ ḥasan*), Abū Dāwūd and Nasāʾī.

[16] Narrated by Bukhārī and al-Ḥākim.

[17] Narrated by Bukhārī, Muslim, Nasāʾī and Abū Dāwūd.

[18] Narrated by Abū Dāwūd, Nasāʾī and Ibn Ḥibbān.

[19] Narrated by Bukhārī, Muslim, Tirmidhī (who graded it *hasan ṣaḥīḥ*), Abū Dāwūd and Ibn Mājah.

tell him: The Messenger of God commands you not to kill [women and] children, nor hired workers".[20]

8. Ibn 'Abbās says: The Messenger of God, when dispatching his troops, would tell them, "[...] Do not behave treacherously, nor misappropriate war-booty, nor mutilate [those whom you kill], nor kill children, nor the people in cloisters".[21]

   Another version contains, " [...] Do not kill a decrepit old man, nor a child, nor a youngster, nor a woman [...]"[22] while two others contain "[...] Do not kill a woman, nor a child, nor an old, aged man [...]"[23] and "Do not kill a child, nor a woman, nor an old man, nor obliterate a stream, nor cut a tree [...]".[24]

9. The words of anyone after the Prophet Muhammad ﷺ do not carry independent religious authority, but his teachings are clearly reflected in the practice of his immediate successor, the first Caliph, Abū Bakr. Abū Bakr gave ten directions to Yazīd ibn Abī Sufyān, one of his commanders, when dispatching him at the head of an army to the Levant:

   "Do not kill any woman, child, or infirm aged person; do not cut down a fruit-bearing tree; do not destroy a dwelling; do not injure a sheep or camel, unless [you need to kill it] for food; neither burn

[20] Narrated by Aḥmad, Ibn Mājah, Taḥāwī and others.

[21] Narrated by Aḥmad, Tirmidhī (who graded it *hasan ṣaḥīḥ*). Shawkānī says, "Its *isnād* contains Ibrahīm ibn Ismā'īl ibn Abi Ḥabībah, who is weak, but Aḥmad regarded him as reliable". The *Muḥaddith* (Ḥadīth master) Zafar Aḥmad 'Uthmanī adds, "'Ijlī also said, "he is a reliable Ḥijazī", as in *al-Tahdhīb* (1/104), and the disagreement is of no detriment, and so the ḥadīth is *ḥasan*". See *I'la al-Sunan*, 12/31.

[22] Narrated by Abū Dāwūd. Shawkānī says, "Its isnād contains Khalid ibn al-Fizr, and he is not that [strong]". 'Uthmani graded it as *ḥasan*, observing that Khalid ibn al-Fizr is rated as "acceptable" in *al-Taqrīb* (p. 51), "a shaykh" by Abū Ḥātim as in *al-Tahdhīb*, and accredited by Ibn Ḥibbān. See *I'la al-Sunan*, 12/31.

[23] Narrated by Baghawī, through his isnād See *Sharḥ al-Sunna*, 11/11. He said, "This is an authentic ḥadīth, narrated by Muslim". It may be observed that Baghawī's wording is more detailed than Muslim's, the latter mentioning only children.

24 Narrated by Bayhaqī, who said, "Its isnād is weak, but it is strengthened by attesting narrations". (See *I'la al-Sunan,* 12/31). Among the supporting narrations is that which Aḥmad has narrated—through a chain containing mediocrity (on account of Ibn Lahi'ah, who is upright but weak in memory) as well as an unnamed narrator:— "Whoever kills a youngster or an old person, or burns a date-palm, or cuts down a fruit-bearing tree, or kills a sheep for its skin, will not return sufficed".

nor submerge a date-palm; do not act unfaithfully [in regard to war-booty]; and do not be cowardly".[25]

A CLARIFICATION ON JIHAD

Jihad is an Arabic noun, coming from the verb meaning to strive to the utmost. There are various types of religious striving, each of which is a type of jihad.

1. Striving to overcome one's own evil tendencies, to fight against Satan's evil prompting, and to purify one's self.

   Verily, Satan is an enemy to you, so take him as an enemy. (Qur'ān, 35:6)

   The Prophet Muhammad ﷺ said, "The *mujāhīd* [26] is the one who strives against his self".[27]

2. Serving one's parents can be a form of jihad.

   A man once came to ask the Prophet's permission to go to battle. He then enquired if the man's parents were alive, and upon learning that they were, told him, "Then perform jihad in their midst [by taking care of them well]".[28]

25 Narrated by Mālik. Qāḍī Shawkānī said, "It is discontinuous". However, it is known that the discontinuous narrations of Mālik's *Muwatta'* can all be found continuously narrated elsewhere, and are regarded as reliable by Mālik, as pointed out by 'Uthmani, and others. See for example, Dihlawi, *Hujjat Allāh al-Bālighah,* 1/249; 'Umari, *Bu ḥūth fi Tarikh al-Sunnah al-Musharrafah,* 242; 'Uthmani, *I'la al-Sunan,* 12/25.

26 *Mujāhid* means "one who performs jihad".

27 Tirmidhī (*hasan ṣaḥīḥ*), Aḥmad and Ibn Ḥibbān.

28 Narrated with the wording, "Then perform jihad in their midst", by Bukhārī, Muslim, Tirmidhī (*hasan ṣaḥīḥ*), Nasā'ī, Abū Dāwūd, Ibn Mājah and Aḥmad. Another version, recorded by Muslim, says that the Prophet ﷺ asked him, "Do you desire the reward from God?" and that when the man replied in the affirmative, he told him, "Then go back to your parents and keep good companionship with them". Another version, with Nasā'ī, Ibn Majah and Aḥmad, says that the man mentioned that he had left behind his parents crying, whereupon the Prophet ﷺ told him, "Then go back to them, and make them smile as you have made them cry". Another version with Aḥmad has the same wording, with the addendum, "And [the Prophet] refused to accept his pledge [to fight]". The chain of narration of this set of narrations is common, and contains 'Aṭā' ibn al-Sā'ib, who was a reliable narrator except that his memory deteriorated in old age. A version with Aḥmad has, "Then go back and show kindness to your parents". Its narrators are reliable, except that Muhammad ibn Ishāq used to commit *tadlis,* and Yazīd ibn Abi Ḥabib used to commit *irsal.*

3. Speaking out against evil in one's society.

   "The best jihad is to speak a true word before a tyrant ruler".[29]

4. Conveying the message of Islam.

   Invite to the way of your Sustainer with wisdom, and excellent exhortation, and dispute with them in the best way. (Qur'ān, 16:125)

   Therefore, do not obey the non-Muslims [regarding your religion], *but strive against them, with* [the Qur'ān], *a great striving.* (Qur'ān, 25:52)[30]

   The striving here refers to conveying the message of Islam peaceably, for there is general agreement that this verse was revealed in Makka[31], and there is no disagreement that warfare was prohibited for Muslims in the Makkan era.

5. Striving in a just war, for the right reasons, either on the battlefield, or through some other assistance.

   "Perform jihad against the pagans with your wealth, your selves and your tongues".[32]

   It should be noted that this text is not a call, let alone a justification, for Muslims to attack each and every non-Muslim. There are very specific circumstances in which warfare can be justified, and even

Note: *Tadlīs* and *irsāl* are technical terms in ḥadīth methodology, and their meaning is as follows: X has committed *tadlīs* if X has met Y, but narrates from him some ḥadīth which he has not heard directly from him, and yet does not mention any intermediaries, giving the impression of direct transmission. X has committed *irsāl* if he was from the second generation after the Prophet Muhammad ﷺ, such that he did not meet him, and yet narrates ḥadīth which he attributes directly to the Prophet, without mentioning any intermediary between. Both *irsāl* and *tadlīs* are among the sources of lesser weakness in a single narration, but the doubt introduced can be effectively dismissed if other, independent, supporting narrations exist. See, for further discussion: M. M. Aẓamī, *Studies in Ḥadīth Methodology and Literature,* 58–67; Qārī, *Sharḥ Sharḥ Nukhbat al-Fikar,* pp. 399–423. From the preceding details, it appears that the wording cited in the main text is most reliable. It should also be noted that in a dire situation, such as when one's own city is under attack, one could (and actually should) go and defend the city even if the parents disapprove, as indicated by another narration.

[29] Tirmidhī (*ḥasan gharib*), Abū Dāwūd, Nasā'ī, Ibn Mājah and Aḥmad.

[30] The commentary on this verse is examined in David Dakake's essay in this collection.

[31] See for example: Suyuṭi's *al-Itqān,* 1/17, Ālūsī's *Rūḥ al-Mā'anī,* 19/49, Qurṭubī's *Al-Jāmī' li-Ahkām al-Qur'ān,* 13/3 and 13/56.

[32] Abū Dāwūd; Nasā'ī, Aḥmad and Dārimī.

then the aim is not to annihilate one's opponents. It is important to view texts such as this ḥadīth within their original historical context, as well as within the context of the complete corpus of relevant sacred texts.

WHEN IS WARFARE JUSTIFIED?

This brings us to the question: What constitutes a just war for Muslims? Combat is not to be sought after for its own sake. The Prophet Muhammad ﷺ said,

"O people! Do not wish for an encounter with the enemy, and ask God for well-being, but when you encounter them be steadfast".[33]

Islam strictly regulates when war is permitted, as well as how it must be undertaken when it is unavoidable. During the early part of the Prophet Muhammad's message, while he preached in his birthplace of Makka, he and his followers were prohibited from fighting, as referred to previously:

Have you not seen those who were told, 'Restrain your hands [from warfare], *and establish the prayer and give the purifying charity?'* (Qur'ān 4:77)

This period lasted for thirteen years, and the prohibition was observed in spite of the fact that the early Muslims were persecuted severely, so much so that those who were able eventually emigrated to Abyssinia and Medina. The religion continued to develop with ongoing revelation of the Divine Law during the Prophet's lifetime, and fighting was later permitted. The following are the causes for which Islam allows fighting:

1. Fighting in self-defence, to thwart an act of aggression, which has been committed, or is clearly about to be committed.

   And fight, in the path of God, those who fight you. (Qur'ān, 2:190)

2. Fighting in response to injustice and oppression.

   Permission is given to those who fight because they have been wronged. (Qur'ān, 22:39)

   Had it not been for God's countering some people by means of others, the earth would surely have become decadent. (Qur'ān, 2:251)

[33] Bukhārī and Muslim.

3. Fighting to secure religious freedom for oppressed Muslims, or to reinstate freedom and calm to allow people in general to become informed about Islam and then make their choice of religion without persecution for it.

   What is the matter with you, that you do not fight in the path of God, and [for the sake] *of the oppressed from among the men, women and children who say: Our Sustainer! Deliver us forth from this city, whose people are oppressors*!? (Qur'ān, 4:75)

   And fight them until there is no more persecution. (Qur'ān, 8:39)

   Muslims may not, however, force people to convert to Islam. History and Islamic sacred texts testify to the peaceful coexistence of non-Muslims in Muslim societies.

   [Let there be] *no compulsion in religion.* (Qur'ān, 2:256)

Islam teaches that the human being has been given free will, to choose whether or not to submit to the truth and to obey his Creator, and in the Afterlife people will be brought to account and judged for their choices. Islam lays great stress on personal accountability, emphasizes the importance of truth, and teaches that an honest seeker can recognize the truth. However, this world is considered the abode of testing, and a forced conversion is antithetical to the concept of testing. The Hereafter is the abode of recompense, wherein evil and rejection will be punished by a just God.

REGULATIONS OF WARFARE

Even in conditions in which war is justified, Islam constrains the fighting within clear ethical and humane guidelines, most prominent of which are the following:

1. The intention should be solely for the sake of God, not for fame, glory, wealth or goods, nor to merely further personal ambition or power.

   A man asked the Prophet Muhammad ﷺ what constitutes fighting in the path of God, saying, "A man may fight out of rage, or [merely] out of bravery, or to show off". The Prophet Muhammad

ﷺ replied, "Whoever fights in order that the word of God should be highest, he is in the path of God".[34]

Among the people with whom Hell will be kindled on the Day of Judgment will be a man who fought in a just war, but did so to gain a reputation as a brave soldier rather than fighting for the sake of God.[35]

2. Reasonable initiatives for peace are to be heeded, and fighting must stop if the enemy desists from hostility.

   And, if they incline towards peace then incline [you also] *towards it.* (Qur'ān, 8:61)

   If they desist, then let there be no enmity except toward the oppressors. (Qur'ān, 2:193)

   The wars between the Muslims and the Romans started when the latter declared war by killing an envoy of the Prophet. Despite this initiation of hostility, the Prophet Muhammad ﷺ, upon dispatching his troops to the battle of Mu'tah, the first of the subsequent battles, instructed his army to first invite the enemy to Islam, and not to attack should they accept. Similarly, even if an enemy soldier, who is about to be killed in the midst of battle, utters the declaration of faith in Islam, his life is to be spared, even though he may be insincere. God will judge him according to his intention.

3. Requests for protection and safe passage are to be granted and honoured.

   If one of the pagans seeks your protection, then grant him protection, so that he may hear the word of God, then escort him to a place of safety. (Qur'ān, 9:6)

   Umm Hānī, a female, Muslim cousin of the Prophet, once gave a pledge of protection to a non-Muslim man, but feared that this guarantee might not be respected. The Prophet told her, "We have

[34] Muslim, Bukhārī, Abū Dāwūd, Tirmidhī (*ḥasan ṣaḥīḥ*) and Ibn Mājah.
[35] Muslim, Tirmidhī (*ḥasan gharīb*), Nasā'ī and Aḥmad.

granted protection to whom you have granted protection, O Umm Hānī".[36]

The Prophet Muhammad ﷺ granted diplomatic immunity even to the envoy of a hostile government which he viewed as illegitimate; that of Musaylimah the false prophet.[37]

4. Non-combatants, such as women and children, may not be targeted.

   And fight, in the path of God, those who fight you, and do not transgress limits. (Qur'ān, 2:190)

   Ribāḥ ibn al-Rabīʿ al-Tamīmī, one of the Prophet's companions, says, "We were with the Messenger of God in a battle. He saw people gathered, and then he saw a slain woman, whereupon he said, 'This [woman] was not fighting!'"[38] Another version adds, "Thereupon, the Prophet objected to the killing of women and children".[39]

5. When it becomes necessary to kill an enemy soldier, the killing should be done in the most humane way possible, and the body should not be mutilated, whether before or after killing. Tactics such as communal starvation are also inhumane and unethical. Prisoners of war are to be treated well.

   "The most restrained people in killing are the people of True Faith (*īmān*)".[40]

   "The Messenger of God used to encourage us to give charity, and used to forbid us from mutilation".[41]

   Charity is positive, contributing to the building of society, whereas mutilation is destructive and pointless. The Muslim is meant to strive to be a positive and constructive influence on the world.

[36] Bukhārī and Muslim.

[37] Abū Dāwūd.

[38] Narrated by Abū Dāwūd, Nasā'ī and Ibn Ḥibbān.

[39] Narrated by Bukhārī, Muslim, Tirmidhī (who graded it *ḥasan ṣaḥīḥ*), Abū Dāwūd and Ibn Mājah.

[40] Abū Dāwūd, Ibn Mājah and Aḥmad.

[41] Bukhārī.

Mutilating bodies and targeting civilians are not only unjustified, but also sow resentment and bitterness in the hearts and minds of people on the other side. This is not what Islam wants. Islam seeks the welfare of mankind, and to endear itself to people so that they will be receptive to it and hence benefit from it.

We have sent you [O Muhammad] *only as a mercy to all creation.* (Qur'ān 21:107)

6. It is not permissible to destroy property, kill animals, cut down trees or burn dwellings (when not dictated by dire necessity), for such actions are forms of corruption.

Among mankind is he whose speech impresses you in worldly life, and he calls God to witness as to what is in his heart, yet he is the fiercest of opponents. And, when he goes away, he strives throughout the land to cause corruption therein, and to destroy crops and lives. And God does not love corruption. (Qur'ān, 2:204–5)

7. It is not permissible to plunder.

"The Messenger of God forbade plundering and mutilation".[42]

After one of the battles in the time of the Prophet, a man was found killed in combat. People started to say, "He is a martyr," but the Prophet told them, "He is in the Fire [of Hell] because of a garment which he misappropriated".[43]

8. It is prohibited to break pledges, or to behave treacherously.

The Prophet ﷺ used to instruct his forces, before dispatching them, "[...] do not behave treacherously [...]".[44]

"When a man has confidence in another man, and then he kills him after he had confidence in him, a banner of treachery will be hoisted for him on the Day of Resurrection".[45]

[42] Bukhārī.
[43] Muslim, Tirmidhī (*ḥasan ṣaḥīḥ gharib*) and Aḥmad.
[44] Aḥmad and Tirmidhī (*ḥasan ṣaḥīḥ*).
[45] Ḥākim, who judged it authentic, and was corroborated by Dhahabī.

9. Forgiveness and other higher moral values are also stressed. The Prophet Muhammad ﷺ once forgave a man who tried to assassinate him in his sleep.[46] He also forgave a group of 70–80 would-be assassins who were apprehended by his men at Tan'im.[47] He forgave a Jewish woman who tried to poison him.[48] And, when he re-entered his birthplace of Makka in triumph, after years of persecution by its inhabitants and years of exile, he granted a general amnesty to its people, his former bitter enemies and antagonists.[49]

10. Finally, we may note that war is in the realm of government affairs, and as such can only be declared by a legitimate Islamic government. The individual does not have the right to assume this responsibility, unless he is under direct attack, in which case he may obviously defend himself against the attacker.

MARTYRS

Fighting and risking one's life for a just cause, for the greater good of people, is a noble endeavour. One who is doing this sincerely and purely for the sake of God, with true and correct faith, is indeed to be commended, and has performed the highest form of jihad. Human beings themselves feel the desire to decorate and honour people who they feel have died in such a cause. Surely, God is more just in rewarding, and more generous. The fact that God rewards a martyr is then quite comprehensible, and is not to be taken (as some attempt to portray it) as a glorification of warfare for its own sake, especially in light of the stringent Islamic regulations we have already mentioned.

Do not think those who were killed in the Path of God to be dead. Nay, they are alive, receiving sustenance from their Creator. (Qur'ān, 3:169–70)

We may also note that the Prophet ﷺ has listed numerous other ways in which a Muslim can achieve martyrdom, although the martyr of the battlefield has a higher rank. He said, "Martyrs are seven [categories] other

[46] Bukhārī.

[47] Muslim, Tirmidhī (*ḥasan ṣaḥīḥ*), Abū Dāwūd and Aḥmad.

[48] Muslim.

[49] Ibn Sa'd.

than being killed in the Path of God: The one who dies in plague is a martyr, the one who drowns is a martyr, the one who dies of a lung inflammation is a martyr, the one who dies of a stomach ailment is a martyr, one who dies in a fire is a martyr, the one who dies under the collapse of a building is a martyr, a woman who dies after delivery [of a child] is a martyr".[50]

EPILOGUE

Islam does not preach indiscriminate antagonism or blind hatred towards non-Muslims. Warfare is permitted only under certain compelling circumstances, and is guided by strict regulations. Muslims are to wish people well in general, and are obligated to share Islam with them, out of a hope that they would embrace it and thereby benefit themselves by it. However, while he can wish and pray for their conversion, he cannot force them. Even if they do not embrace Islam, a Muslim is still to deal kindly and justly with them, more so if they are his relatives or neighbours.[51] The following verse summarizes the normal state of relations between Muslims and non-Muslims.

God does not prohibit you from being kind and just to those who have not fought you on account of religion, nor expelled you from your homes. God loves those who are just. (Qur'ān 60:8)

[50] Narrated in this form by Mālik. Bukhārī, Muslim, Nasā'ī, Tirmidhī (*ḥasan ṣaḥīḥ*), Ibn Mājah and Aḥmad have reported the ḥadīth with five categories. It may be noted that Bukhārī quoted Mālik's version (7 categories) in his chapter heading, but then cited the version of the ḥadīth which mentions 5 categories. There is no contradiction, as discussed by Hafiz ibn Hajar in *Fatḥ al-Barī*(6/51-52). He mentions that actually more than twenty forms of martyrdom can be collected from different soundly transmitted ḥadīths. One *ḥasan* ḥadīth even says that every death a Muslim dies is martyrdom. Of course, there are different levels of martyrdom, the most superior being that of being killed in the Path of God, since the voluntary sacrifice made there is greatest.

[51] The Prophet Muhammad ﷺ has said, "By God, he does not have [proper] faith [...] he whose neighbor is not safe from his mischief". (Bukhārī) He also said, "Gabriel continued to advise me concerning [rights of] the neighbour, until I thought he would make him inherit". (Bukhārī and Muslim)

6 The Myth of a Militant Islam

DAVID DAKAKE

IN THE POST 9/11 environment there is an urgent need for a clear enunciation of the views of traditional Islam in regard to jihad, so-called "holy war". The first matter which needs to be made clear is that jihad is not simply fighting or holy warfare. In Arabic, jihad literally means "effort", that is, to exert oneself in some way or another. Within the context of Islam, jihad has the meaning of exerting oneself for the sake of God, and this exertion can be in an infinite number of ways, from giving charity and feeding the poor, to concentrating intently in one's prayers, to controlling one's self and showing patience and forgiveness in the face of offenses, to gaining authentic knowledge, to physical fighting to stop oppression and injustice. Generally speaking, anything that requires something of us—that is, requires that we go beyond the confines of our individual ego and desires—or anything that we bear with or strive after for the sake of pleasing God can be spoken of as a "jihad" in Islam.[1] This understanding of jihad is such that when the "five pillars"[2] of the faith are

[1] As regards women, for example, there are ḥadīth that declare that the "jihad of women" is making the pilgrimage (*ḥājj*) to Makka. See Bukhārī, *Ṣaḥīḥ Bukhārī* (Medina: Dār al-Fikr, n.d.), vol. 4, pp. 36, 83–84 (*Kitāb al-jihad*, ḥadīth n. 43, 127, 128). There are also ḥadīth concerning the various types of death that qualify one as a martyr (*shahīd*), i.e., as having died like a fighter in jihad. One such type of death is said to be the death of a woman in childbirth. Other traditions in *Ṣaḥīḥ al-Bukhārī* imply that women can fulfil the duty of jihad by attending to the wounded on the battlefield (see *Saḥīḥ* vol. 4, pp. 86–87, ḥadīth n. 131–134). See also Muslim, *Ṣaḥīḥ Muslim* (printed with commentaries) (Beirut: Dār al-Kutub al-'Ilmiyya, 1978), vol. 5, pp. 153, 157.

[2] These are: 1) testifying that there is only one true God and that Muhammad ﷺ is His messenger, 2) praying five times a day, 3) paying a charity-tax every year, 4) fasting during the month of Ramaḍān, and 5) making a pilgrimage to Makka once in one's life, if one has the means and the health to do so.

taught, jihad is sometimes classified as a "sixth pillar" which pervades the other five, representing an attitude or intention that should be present in whatever one does for the sake of God.

This being said, there is no doubt that jihad has an important martial aspect. To understand this we should remember that within the Islamic tradition the term "jihad" has been understood to possess two poles: an outward pole and an inward pole. These two poles are illustrated in the words of the Prophet Muhammad ﷺ when he said to his companions, after they had returned from a military campaign in defense of the Medinan community: "We have returned from the lesser (*asghar*) jihad to the greater (*akbar*) jihad".[3] Here the lesser jihad refers to physical fighting, whereas having come back to the relative physical safety of their city of Medina, the Muslims faced yet a greater jihad—namely, the struggle against the passionate, carnal soul that constantly seeks its own self-satisfaction above all else, being forgetful of God. This famous saying of the Prophet emphasises the hierarchy of the two types of jihad, as well as the essential "balance" that must be maintained between its outward and inward forms,[4] a balance often neglected in the approach of certain modern Islamic groups that seek to reform people and society from "without", forcing change in the outward behavior of men and women without first bringing about a sincere change in their hearts and minds. This is the lesson of the words of the Qur'ān when God says, *We never change the state of a people until they change themselves.* (Qur'ān 13:11)[5] This lesson, as we shall see when we examine the earliest military jihad, was not lost on the first Muslims.

In the present crisis, the pronouncements of many self-styled Middle East "experts" and Muslim "authorities" who have dealt with the subject of jihad have generally been of two kinds. There have been those who have sought, in a sense, to brush aside the whole issue and history of military

[3] See 'Aljunī, *Kashf al-khafā'* (Beirut: Dār Iḥyā' al-Turāh al-'Arabī, 1968), ḥadīth n. 1362.

[4] It should be noted that "outward jihad" is by no means only military in nature. The arena of outward jihad is the level of human action. It is not concerned with inner attitudes of the soul, such as sincerity and love (which constitute the realm of the inner jihad) but with proper outward action alone, as defined by the religious law (*sharī'a*).

[5] The word translated here as "themselves", *anfusihim* in Arabic, may be more literally translated as "their souls". This demonstrates an essential Qur'ānic perspective: the inner struggle (i.e., "until they change *their souls*") takes precedence over the outer struggle (i.e., the particular state in which a people exist at the moment) and furthermore, that no amount of purely outward actions can overcome hypocrisy of soul.

jihad in Islam in favor of a purely spiritualised notion of "striving" in the way of God; and there have been those, both Muslim and non-Muslim, who have provided literal or surface readings of Qur'ānic verses related to jihad and "fighting" (*qitāl*) in an attempt to reduce all of Islam to military jihad.[6] The first view represents an apologetic attitude that attempts to satisfy Western notions of non-violence and political correctness but, in so doing, provides an "understanding" that lacks any real relationship to the thought of the majority of Muslim peoples throughout Islamic history. The second view, which would make Islam synonymous with "warfare", is the result either of sheer ignorance or of political agendas that are served by the perpetuation of animosity between peoples. This second position ignores entirely the commentary and analysis of the Islamic intellectual tradition that has served for over one thousand years as a key for Muslims to understand Qur'ānic pronouncements related to jihad. In this essay we will neither water down the analysis of jihad to suit those modernists who oppose any notions of legitimate religious struggle and conflict, nor disregard, as do the "fundamentalists", the intellectual and spiritual heritage of Islam which has defined for traditional Muslims the validity, but also the limitations, of the lesser jihad.

In carrying out this study we propose to examine those verses of the Qur'ān that deal with fighting, as well as those which define those who are to be fought against in jihad. We will also provide, along with this textual analysis of Qur'ānic doctrines of war, an historical analysis of the actual forms of the earliest jihad and the conduct of the *mujāhidūn*, the fighters in jihad, as exemplified by the Prophet Muhammad ﷺ and his successors, the "Rightly-guided Caliphs", given that their actions have served for Muslims as an indispensable example to clarify Qur'ānic pronouncements.[7] In this way, we hope to avoid both the etherialization of jihad by Muslim apologists, and the distortion of the tradition at the

[6] There are a few important exceptions to this categorisation. Among them are the articles of Khaled Abou El Fadl, "The Place of Tolerance in Islam", in the book by the same title, Eds. J. Cohen and I. Lague (Beacon Press, 2002), "The Rules of Killing at War: An Inquiry into the Classical Sources", *Muslim World* 89, no. 2 (April 1999), and Sherman Jackson, "Jihad and the Modern World", *The Journal of Islamic Law and Culture* (Spring/Summer 2002).

[7] For examples of how these traditional teachings were followed in later generations see Reza Shah-Kazemi's "Recollecting the Spirit of Jihad" in Joseph E. B. Lumbard ed., *Islam, Fundamentalism, and the Betrayal of Tradition* (World Wisdom Books, 2004).

hands of the "fundamentalists". Lastly, we will examine "fundamentalist" interpretations of jihad and compare them with the traditional understanding of jihad in the early Qur'ānic commentaries and the actual history of Islam.

"DO NOT TAKE CHRISTIANS AND JEWS AS *AWLIYĀ'*"

Following the events of 9/11 there is one verse of the Qur'ān which has often been quoted by radio announcers, talk-show hosts, and "fundamentalists" in both the East and the West. Before we deal with the actual issue of warfare or military jihad, it is necessary to say something about this verse which, if not understood correctly, can bias any further discussions. This verse appears in chapter 5, verse 51 of the Qur'ān:

> *O, you who believe* [in the message of Muhammad], *do not take Jews and Christians as awliyā'. They are awliyā' to one another, and the one among you who turns to them is of them. Truly, God does not guide wrongdoing folk.*

The word *awliyā'* (sing. *walī*), which we left above in the original Arabic, has been commonly translated into English as "friends".[8] Given this translation, the verse appears to be a very clear statement opposing what we might term "normative" or "kindly relations" between Muslims and non-Muslims; but when we look at the traditional Qur'ānic commentaries of medieval times, which discuss the events surrounding the revelation of this verse, the modern translation becomes suspect. But before examining this issue in depth, it is necessary to clarify the importance of "verse context" in the Qur'ān. Here a comparison between the Biblical text and the Qur'ān is helpful.

Comparing the Bible and the Qur'ān, we can use certain images to illustrate some of the major stylistic differences between the two sacred scriptures. We could say, for example, that the Bible is like a "flowing stream"; when one reads the text there is a constant contextualization of the various verses, stories, chapters, and books. One begins reading with the story of Genesis, the creation of the world and the first man and woman, and then proceeds on through time, moving into the stories of the

[8] Although it is incorrect in this context, the six major translations of the Qur'ān available in English, those of A. J. Arberry, Marmaduke Pickthall, N. J. Dawood, Yusuf Ali, Ahmad Ali, and El-Hilali/Khan, all translate the word *awliyā'* as "friends".

early patriarchs, then the later Hebrew judges and prophets, the coming of Christ, the post-Jesus community of the Apostles, and finally the end of the world in the Book of Revelation. As one reads the Bible there is a historical context established for each of the major stories and events which enables the reader to situate what is being said within time and space, and indeed priority. The orientation of events as related to the chapters and verses is made explicit through the historical "flow" of the stories and, in the case of the New Testament, the eventual culmination of the text and all history.

In contrast, if we were to use an image to illustrate the Qur'ānic revelation, it would be that of an individual standing upon a mountain at night as lightning flashes on him and in a valley below.[9] As this individual looks out upon the landscape shrouded in darkness, he would see sudden flashes, sudden illuminations of different portions of the mountain and the valley, but there would not appear to be any immediate relationship between these different illuminated regions, surrounded as they are by vast shadows. Of course, a relationship does exist between the different areas illuminated by the lightning, but that relationship is not explicit. It is hidden amid the darkness. This is something like the situation that is faced by the reader upon first examining the Qur'ān. One will often read sections of the text and wonder what is the relationship between the various pronouncements that one encounters, for the Qur'ān does not tell "stories" as the Western reader is accustomed to from the Biblical tradition. In fact, there is only one "full-length" story in the Qur'ānic text, in the chapter on the prophet Joseph ﷺ. The rest of the Qur'ān is a series of verses grouped into chapters and sections, and often two verses right next to one another will actually refer to two completely different events in the life of the early Islamic community. It is for this reason that the Qur'ānic commentary tradition (*Tafsīr*) deals so extensively with what is known in Arabic as *asbāb al-nuzūl*, or the occasions for God revealing particular Qur'ānic verses. Without reference to these "occasions" of revelation most of the verses of the Qur'ān would be susceptible to any and all forms of interpretation. This issue of the need for knowledge of the commentary tradition is, of course, further complicated—for those unable to read the original Arabic text—by

[9] We owe this image to Dr. Seyyed Hossein Nasr.

translations, which often add yet another layer of difficulty for coming to terms with the meaning of the verses. When we examine verse 5:51, we encounter both these problems of context and translation.

The difficulties in understanding verse 5:51 begin with the translation of the Arabic word awliyā', commonly rendered as "friends". In the context of this verse, the word awliyā' does not mean "friends" at all, as we use the term in English, and we know this from examining the occasion for its revelation. While it is true that awliyā' can mean "friends", it has additional meanings such as "guardians", "protectors", and even "legal guardians". When we consult the traditional commentaries on the Qur'ān, we are told that this verse was revealed at a particularly delicate moment in the life of the early Muslim community. To understand this verse it is thus necessary to explain the existential situation of the Muslims at this time in Arabia.

Before 5:51 was revealed, the Prophet Muhammad ﷺ and the Muslims had only recently migrated as a community from Makka to Medina, some 400 kilometers to the north. They had done so, according to Islamic histories, due to the persecution to which they were subjected at the hands of their fellow tribesmen and relatives in Makka. Most Makkans worshipped many idols as "gods" and feared the rising interest in the message of the Prophet Muhammad ﷺ within the city, even though he was himself a son of Makka. The Makkans feared the growing presence of the Muslims amongst them because the Muslims claimed that there was only one true God, who had no physical image, and who required of men virtue, generosity, and fair and kind treatment of the weaker members of society. This simple message, in fact, threatened to overturn the order of Makkan society, based as it was upon the worship of multiple gods and the privilege of the strong and the wealthy. It also threatened to disrupt the economic benefits of this privilege, the annual pilgrimage season, when peoples from all over Arabia would come to worship their many idols/gods at the Ka'ba—a cubical structure which the Qur'ān claims was originally built by Abraham and his son Ishmael (peace be upon them) as a temple to the one God, before the decadence of religion in Arabia.[10] The message of Islam threatened to replace the social and economic system of Makkan polytheism with the worship of the one God, Who—as in the stories of the Old Testament—would not allow that others be

[10] Qur'ān 2:125–129.

worshiped alongside Him. In this difficult environment the Prophet Muhammad ﷺ preached peacefully the message of monotheism and virtue, but he and his small band of followers were eventually driven from the city by torture, embargo, threats of assassination, and various other forms of humiliation and abuse. The Muslims then migrated to Medina where the Prophet Muhammad ﷺ had been invited to come and live in safety with his followers and where the main Arab tribes of the city had willingly accepted his message and authority.

According to one of the earliest and most famous Qur'ānic commentators, al-Ṭabarī (839–923 CE/225–310 AH), it was not long after this migration to Medina that verse 5:51 was revealed. Specifically, al-Ṭabarī tells us that this verse came down around the time of the battle of Badr (623 CE/2 AH) or perhaps after the battle of Uhud (625 CE/3 AH).[11] In these early days the Muslim community constituted no more than a few hundred people and had already left the city of Makka; yet the Makkans continued to attempt to confront them militarily, and these two early battles, as well as others, were crucial events in the history of the early Islamic community. Militarily, the Makkans were a far more powerful force than the Muslims and they had allies throughout Arabia. Given the small numbers of the Muslims, the Prophet and his fledgling community faced the real possibility of utter annihilation should they lose any of these early conflicts. Al-Ṭabarī tells us that within this highly charged environment some members of the Muslim community wanted to make individual alliances with other non-Muslim tribes in the region. Within Medina there were Jewish tribes who constituted a powerful presence in the town and who were on good terms with the Makkans, and to the north of the city there were also Christian Arab tribes. Some Muslims saw the possibility of making alliances with one or more of these groups as a way of guaranteeing their own survival should the Makkan armies ultimately triumph. This was the stark reality of Arabia at that time; it was only through the protection of one's tribe or alliances with other tribes or clans that one's individual security was insured.

From the perspective of Islam, however, the Prophet Muhammad ﷺ realized that a young community, faced with great peril, could not allow such "dissension" in the ranks of the faithful as would be created by

[11] Al-Ṭabarī, *Jāmiʿ al-bayān ʿan taʾwīl āy al-Qurʾān* (Beirut: Dār al-Fikr, 1995), vol. 4, pp. 372–373.

various individuals making bonds of loyalty with other groups not committed to the Islamic message. Indeed, from the Islamic point of view such actions, had they been allowed, would have been a kind of communal suicide that would have seriously undermined Muslim unity, broken the morale of the community (*umma*), and perhaps caused the many individuals making such alliances to lack fortitude in the face of danger.

Bearing these historical issues in mind, it becomes obvious that the translation of awliyā' as "friends" is incorrect. It should be rendered, in accord with another of its traditional Arabic meanings, as "protectors" or "guardians" in the strict military sense of these terms. The verse should be read as, "Do not take Christians and Jews as your protectors. They are protectors to one another [...]". This is the true message of the verse, and the appropriateness of this understanding is supported by the fact that the Qur'ān does not oppose simple kindness between peoples, as is clear from verse 60:8, to which we shall now turn.

"TO DEAL KINDLY AND JUSTLY"

Verse 60:8 says, *God does not forbid that you should deal kindly and justly with those who do not fight you for the sake of* [your] *religion or drive you out of your homes. Truly, God loves those who are just.* Al-Ṭabarī tells us that this verse was revealed on the occasion of an incident involving the half-sister of one of the Prophet's wives.[12] According to him, Asmā' bint Abī Bakr, who was a Muslim living in Medina, received some gifts from her mother, Qutaylah, who lived in Makka. Qutaylah had refused to convert to Islam and continued to practice the idolatrous ways of the Makkans. Asmā' said, upon receiving the gifts, that she would not accept them, given that they came from one who had rejected the message of Islam and indeed one who had chosen to live among the arch-enemies of the Muslims; but then the above Qur'ānic verse was revealed to the Prophet ﷺ, indicating that there was no need to be ungracious towards the one who gave these gifts, even though she had rejected the message of the Prophet and was living with the enemies of Islam.

Al-Ṭabarī goes even further in his analysis of the verse by criticizing those Muslims who say that 60:8 was later abrogated by another Qur'ānic verse

[12] Ibid., vol. 14, pp. 83–84.

which says, *Slay the idolaters wheresoever you find them.* (Qur'ān 9:5)[13] Al-Ṭabarī says that the most proper interpretation of verse 60:8 is that God commanded kindness and justice to be shown "amongst all of the kinds of communities and creeds" and did not specify by His words some communities to the exclusion of others. Al-Ṭabarī says that here God speaks in general of any group that does not openly fight against the Muslims or drive them out of their homes, and that the opinion that this kindness was abrogated by later Qur'ānic statements makes no sense.[14] This understanding may seem to be in contradiction with our previous statement that the Makkans were indeed at war with the Muslims; however, Qutaylah, being a woman, could not technically be considered a "combatant" according to Islamic law. Indeed, this shows the essential distinction between combatants and non-combatants in the rules of Muslim warfare. This distinction, as we see from the example of Qutaylah, is to be upheld even in the context of engagement with an actively hostile enemy, as were the Makkans. Therefore, Islam does not oppose friendship and kindness between peoples who are not at war with one another and, even in the case of war, clear distinctions are to be made between "those who fight" and "those who do not fight". We shall examine this principle further in the next section.

"SLAY THEM WHERESOEVER YOU FIND THEM"

Another verse that is related to jihad, and also deals with the subject of those against whom jihad is to be waged, is 2:190–191. According to many accounts, this verse represents the first command given by God to the Muslims to carry out military jihad,[15] but this command had specific limitations placed upon it, as we shall see. The Qur'ānic text reads as follows:

> *Fight in the way of God against those who fight you, but transgress not the limits. Truly, God does not love the transgressors* [of limits].

[13] We will look more closely at verse 9:5 when we examine the fatwa of the World Islamic Front later in this essay.

[14] Al-Ṭabarī, vol. 14, p. 84.

[15] Ibid., vol. 2, p. 258. It should be noted that there is another group of verses, 22:39–40 which is also considered to have been the first verses to speak about the military jihad. We shall have occasion to speak about this later in the essay.

> *And slay them wheresoever you find them, and turn them out from where they have turned you out.*

Al-Ṭabarī tells us that this verse is not to be read as a *carte blanche* to attack any and all non-Muslim peoples; rather, he says, the verse was revealed specifically in relation to fighting the idolaters of Makka, who are referred to in Arabic sources by the technical term *mushrikūn* or *mushrikīn* (sing. *mushrik*).[16] This term comes from a three-letter Arabic root "sh-r-k" which means "to associate" or "take a partner unto something", and the word mushrikūn literally means "those who take a partner unto God", that is to say, "polytheists" or "idolaters". It should be noted that from the point of view of Islamic law, this injunction to perform jihad against the polytheists does not pertain to either Jews or Christians. Neither Jews nor Christians are ever referred to within the Qur'ān by the terms mushrik or mushrikūn. They have, in fact, a very different status according to the Qur'ān, which often refers to the two groups together by the technical term *ahl al-kitāb* or "People of the Book", meaning people who have been given a scripture by God other than the Muslims. We shall discuss the status of Jews and Christians later, but what is important to recognise here is that this call to jihad was revealed in relation to a specific group of people, the idolaters of Makka, and within a specific context, a context of persecution and the driving of Muslims from their homes in Makka because of their religion. Indeed, this understanding is accepted not only by al-Ṭabarī but, he says, it is the view of most Qur'ānic interpreters.[17]

In addition to this context for the first military jihad, there were also limits placed upon the early Muslims who carried out jihad against the mushrikūn. Verse 2:190 speaks of "fight[ing] in the way of God" but also of not transgressing the "limits". What are these limits? Al-Ṭabarī gives many accounts detailing the limits placed upon the *mujāhidūn*. He says, for instance, that the cousin of the Prophet Muhammad ﷺ, Ibn 'Abbās, commented upon verse 2:190 as follows: "Do not kill women, or children, or the old, or the one who greets you with peace, or [the one who] restrains his hand [from hurting you], and if you do this

[16] Ibid., vol. 2, p. 258.
[17] Ibid.

then you have transgressed".[18] Another tradition related by al-Ṭabarī comes from the Umayyad Caliph 'Umar ibn 'Abd al-'Azīz or 'Umar II (717/720 CE - 99/101AH), who explained the meaning of 2:191 as: "[...] do not fight he who does not fight you, that is to say women, children, and monks".[19]

These statements quoted by al-Ṭabarī are very much in keeping with other commands given specifically by the Prophet and the Rightly-guided Caliphs (Abū Bakr, 'Umar, 'Uthmān and 'Alī) to the Muslim armies involved in jihad. These commands are noted in the various *ḥadīth* collections, i.e., records of the sayings of the Prophet ﷺ and his companions, which along with the Qur'ān form the basis for determining the Islamic nature of any act. Some examples of these ḥadīth are:

> Nāfi' reported that the Prophet of God ﷺ found women killed in some battles, and he condemned such an act and prohibited the killing of women and children.[20]
>
> When Abu Bakr al-Siddīq [the trusted friend of the Prophet and first of the Rightly-guided Caliphs] sent an army to Syria, he went on foot with Yazīd ibn Abū Sufyān who was the commander of a quarter of the forces .... [Abū Bakr said to him:] "I instruct you in ten matters: Do not kill women, children, the old, or the infirm; do not cut down fruit-bearing trees; do not destroy any town; do not cut the gums of sheep or camels except for the purpose of eating; do not burn date-trees nor submerge them; do not steal from booty and do not be cowardly".[21]
>
> [The Umayyad Caliph] 'Umar ibn 'Abd al-'Azīz wrote to one of his administrators: We have learnt that whenever the Prophet of God ﷺ sent out a force, he used to command them, "Fight, taking the name of the Lord. You are fighting in the cause of the Lord with people who have disbelieved and rejected the Lord. Do not commit theft; do not break vows; do not cut

[18] Ibid., vol. 2, p. 259.

[19] In addition, al-Ṭabarī, reports a second narration of these words of 'Umar ibn 'Abd al-'Azīz with only slight changes in phrasing, Ibid., vol. 2, p. 259.

[20] See Mālik ibn Anas, *Muwaṭṭa'*, trans. M. Rahimuddin (New Delhi: Tāj, 1985), p. 200 (*Kitāb al-jihad*, ḥadīth n. 957). See also Bukhārī, *Ṣaḥīḥ*, vol. 4, pp. 159–160 (*Kitāb al-jihad*, ḥadīth n. 257–258), Abū Dāwūd, *Sunan Abū Dāwūd* (Beirut, Dār al-Kutub al 'Ilmiyya, 1996), vol. 2, p. 258 (*Kitāb al-jihad*, ḥadīth n. 2668), and Muslim, *Ṣaḥīḥ*, vol. 5, p. 56 (*Kitāb al-jihad*).

[21] Mālik, *Muwaṭṭa'*, p. 200 (*Kitāb al-jihad*, ḥadīth n. 958). Other similar instructions are also given to the Muslim armies prohibiting the killing of children and the mutilating of bodies, see Muslim, *Ṣaḥīḥ*, vol. 5, pp. 46–50 (*Kitāb al-jihad*).

ears and noses; do not kill women and children. Communicate this to your armies".[22]

Once when Rabāḥ ibn Rabī'aḥ went forth with the Messenger of God, he and [the] companions of the Prophet passed by a woman who had been slain. The Messenger halted and said: "She is not one who would have fought". Thereupon, he looked at the men and said to one of them: "Run after Khālid Ibn al-Walīd[23] [and tell him] that he must not slay children, serfs, or women".[24]

Such statements are common throughout the ḥadīth collections and leave little doubt as to the limits set upon the military jihad, regardless of the enemy that is faced.

"PERFORM JIHAD AGAINST THE *KĀFIRŪN*"

As we noted earlier, the Qur'ān does not speak of Jews or Christians as mushrikūn or polytheists. Therefore, none of the verses of the Qur'ān that pertain to fighting the mushrikūn pertain to them. However, it must be admitted that the Qur'ān does, within a limited context, speak of Jews and Christians as *Kāfirūn*, a term often translated into English as "unbelievers", although its literal meaning is, "Those who cover over [the truth]" in some form or another. Unfortunately, the common translation of this term as "unbelievers" gives it nuances of meaning from Western cultural history that do not necessarily apply to the original Arabic, such as the fact that "unbelief" in English is synonymous with "atheism". In Arabic, however, *kufr* or "covering" does not necessarily refer to lack of faith but to a lack of correct thinking on one or more aspects of faith. In fact Muslims can also be Kāfirūn. For instance, according to the traditional commentaries, verse 9:49, *There are some who say, 'Give me leave to stay behind and do not tempt me'. Surely they have fallen into temptation already and hell encompasses*

[22] Mālik, *Muwaṭṭa'*, p. 201 (*Kitāb al-jihad*, ḥadīth n. 959). A similar version of this ḥadīth in the *Sunan* of Abū Dāwūd mentions not killing the elderly, in addition to the categories of women and children, see Abū Dāwūd, *Sunan*, vol. 2, p. 243 (*Kitāb al-jihad*, ḥadīth n. 2614).

[23] Khālid ibn al-Walīd (d. 642CE/22AH) was a companion of the Prophet Muhammad ﷺ and one of the famous early commanders of Muslim forces.

[24] Quoted from *Bidāyat al-mujtahid wa nihāyat al-muqtaṣid* of Ibn Rushd, translated by Rudolph Peters in *Jihad in Mediaeval and Modern Islam* (Leiden: E. J. Brill, 1977), p. 17. For a similar version of this ḥadīth see Abū Dāwūd, *Sunan*, vol. 2, p. 258 (*Kitāb al-jihad*, ḥadīth n. 2669).

the unbelievers (Kāfirūn), refers to those Muslims who refused to respond to the Prophet's call to go on an expedition to Tabūk.[25]

The important question that could be asked, however, is: Does not the Qur'ān speak about fighting against the Kāfirūn, such as in the verse: *O Messenger, perform jihad against the unbelievers* (Kāfirūn) *and the hypocrites* (munafiqūn) (Qur'ān 9:73)? Does this verse not imply an essential militancy between Muslims on the one hand, and Jews and Christians on the other? In answering these questions we must refer to both Qur'ānic pronouncements and to the historical actions of the early Muslims in jihad. We will deal with the issues of the Qur'ān first and then turn, in the next section, to what the Muslims actually did in jihad.

When we look at the comments of al-Ṭabarī regarding verse 9:73, as well as those of Ibn Kathīr (d. 1372 CE/774 AH), perhaps the most famous of Sunnī Qur'ān commentators, both seem to condone the idea that this verse relates to violent or military jihad. Both make a distinction, however, between the two types of jihad mentioned in verse 9:73: jihad against the Kāfirūn, and jihad against the munafiqūn. Each states that the jihad against the munafiqūn or hypocrites—i.e., those Muslims who knowingly disobey the commands of God—is "*bi'l-lisān*," meaning "with the tongue". That is to say, one should reprimand the Muslim hypocrites with critical speech, not with physical violence. Whereas, in regard to the Kāfirūn, both commentators make reference to the idea that the jihad against them is "*bi'l-Ṣayf*", or "by the sword".[26] This may seem to suggest that violent suppression of Jews and Christians is demanded, since we have already mentioned that both Jews and Christians—though never called mushrikūn—are sometimes referred to as Kāfirūn. But before drawing this conclusion we must look more closely at how the Qur'ān defines the Kāfirūn. Here it is useful to refer to a series of Qur'ānic verses referring to the "People of the Book", such as 98:1, 98:6, 5:78, and 2:105.

Verse 98:1 reads: *Those who disbelieved* (kafarū) *among* (min) *the People of the Book and the polytheists* (mushrikūn) *would not have left off erring until the clear*

[25] See *Sīrāṭ Rasūl Allāh* of Ibn Isḥāq, trans. by A. Guillaume in *The Life of Muhammad* (Oxford: Oxford University Press, 1978), pp. 602–603.

[26] Al-Ṭabarī, *Jāmi' al-bayān*, vol. 6, pp. 233–234; and Ibn Kathīr, *Tafsīr al-Qur'ān al-'aẓīm* (Riyādh: Dār al-Salām, 1998), vol. 2, pp. 488–489.

truth came to them. This verse clearly indicates that "to disbelieve" is not a characteristic belonging to all Jews and Christians or People of the Book. Instead, it declares that disbelief is a characteristic of some "among" the People of the Book. This limiting of the declaration of unbelief is established by the Arabic preposition *min* within the quotation, which serves to distinguish a distinct species within a genus, namely, those unbelievers present within the larger believing Jewish and Christian communities. This delimitation is also to be seen in verse 98:6 which says, *Those who disbelieved (kafarū) among the People of the Book are in Hell-fire.* Verses 5:78 and 2:105 are yet further examples of this qualifying and limiting of *kufr* or "unbelief" in regard to the People of the Book. They state, respectively:

> *Those who disbelieved* (kafarū) ***among*** *the Tribe of Israel were cursed by the tongue of David and Jesus, son of Mary.* [emphasis added]
>
> *Neither those who disbelieved* (kafarū) ***among*** *the People of the Book, nor the polytheists* (mushrikūn), *love that anything good should be sent down to you from your Lord* [emphasis added]

We see in these verses that the Qur'ānic perspective, as regards the followers of faiths "other than Islam", is a subtle one, not simply a blanket condemnation of all non-Muslims. It is important to recall here the words of verses 113–115 of chapter 3 of the Qur'ān, which say:

> *Not all of them are alike. Of the People of the Book are a group that stand* [in prayer], *rehearse the signs of God throughout the night and prostrate.*
>
> *They believe in God and the Last Day; they enjoin what is right and forbid what is wrong, and they hasten in* [all] *good works. These are among the righteous. Of the good that they do, nothing will be rejected of them, and God knows the God-fearing ones.*

Keeping these Qur'ānic distinctions in mind, the injunction to fight the Kāfirūn "by the sword" does not then apply to all Jews and Christians, but only to some "among" them. But this raises the question, who, among the Jews and Christians, are the Muslims to fight? To answer this question we must now turn to the historical facts of the jihad of the first Muslims.

THE JIHAD OF THE FIRST MUSLIMS

It is perhaps best to begin our discussion of historical jihad by recalling that the first jihad in Islam was not martial and had nothing to do with violence.

The first jihad is referred to in the Qur'ān in verse 25:52, which states, *Do not obey the unbelievers* (Kāfirūn), *but strive against them* (*jāhidhum*) *with it, a great striving*. This somewhat enigmatic verse, traditionally understood to have been revealed at Makka, i.e., before any divine decree had been given as regards performance of military jihad (which came only later in the Medinan period), speaks of striving against the unbelievers by way of "it". Both al-Ṭabarī and Ibn Kathīr relate traditions from Ibn 'Abbās and from Ibn Zayd ibn Hārith, the son of the Prophet's adopted son, telling us that this "it"—the means by which to carry out jihad—is the Qur'ān itself.[27] In other words, the earliest command to jihad was a kind of preaching of the Qur'ān to the Makkans, or perhaps a taking solace or refuge in the Divine Word from the persecutions that the Muslims were experiencing at that time in Makka. It was not military in nature. This brings up our first point regarding the historical form of military jihad and what may be its most misrepresented feature: the notion that the religion of Islam was spread through military force, that Jews, Christians, and other peoples of the Middle East, Asia, and Africa were forced to convert to Islam on pain of death.

"THERE IS NO COMPULSION IN RELIGION"

It has been a common view in the West, even to this day, to say that the religion of Islam spread through conquest. Although this Orientalist theory is now being shown to be a fallacy by modern scholarship,[28] it is important to mention that the peaceful spread of Islam throughout most of the Middle East,[29] Asia, and Africa was in fact due to principles flowing from the

[27] Al-Ṭabarī, *Jāmi' al-bayān*, vol. 11, p. 30; Ibn Kathīr, *Tafsīr*, vol. 3, p. 429.

[28] See for example R. Bulliet, *The Patricians of Nishapur* (Cambridge: Harvard University Press, 1972) and *Islam: The View from the Edge* (New York: Columbia University Press, 1994) where he speaks about the case of the conversion of the Persian plateau. Bulliet has carried out demographic studies showing that for three centuries following the Muslim's political conquest of the region the land of Iran remained a majority Zoroastrian population, in direct contradiction to any notions of forced conversion.

[29] It was only the polytheistic Arab tribes in the Arabian Peninsula who were compelled to enter Islam. Those Arab tribes who were already People of the Book were not forced to accept the religion. Numerous examples of this can be found in the histories, particularly in regard to the Christian Arabs. See the accounts of the Arabs of Najrān (al-Ṭabarī, *Ta'rīkh al-rusul wa'l-mulūk*, Ed. M. J. de Goeje [Leiden: E. J. Brill, 1964], vol. 1, pp. 1987–1988 and p. 2162), the Banū Namir, Banū Iyād, and Banū Taghlib (al- Ṭabarī, *Ta'rīkh*, I, p. 2482 and pp. 2509–2510), the Banū Ghassān (Balādhurī's *Futūḥ al-buldān*, trans., P. Hitti as *The Origins of the Islamic* State [New York: AMS Press], vol. 1, p. 209), the Banū Ṣāliḥ ibn Ḥulwān (Balādhurī, *Origins*, vol. 1, p. 223), the Banū Ṭayyi' and the Arabs of the settlement of Ḥadir Ḥalab (Balādhurī, *Origins*, vol. 1, p. 224), and the Arabs of Ba'labakk (Balādhurī, *Origins*, vol. 1, p. 198).

Qur'ānic revelation itself. Here and in the next section we will discuss some of these principles, beginning with the injunction found in verse 2:256 which says, *There is no compulsion in religion.* Our commentators tell us that this verse was revealed during one of three possible situations.

The first possible context for the revelation of 2:256 has to do with a practice that was fairly common among the women of Medina before Islam came to the city. Our commentators tell us that if a woman did not have any living sons, she would sometimes make a promise that if she gave birth to a child and the child lived, she would raise the child in the faith of one of the Jewish tribes of the city.[30] Apparently this practice was somewhat popular; we know this from the events following another of the early military engagements of Islamic history: the siege of the fortress of the Medinan Jewish tribe of Naḍīr (625 CE/4 AH). The reason for the siege, according to Islamic sources, was that the Banū Naḍīr had broken an alliance that they had concluded with the Prophet Muhammad ﷺ[31] by secretly planning to assassinate him. As a result of this treason, the Muslims besieged the Banū Naḍīr for some ten days in their fortress just south of Medina. At the end of this siege the Banū Naḍīr accepted a punishment of exile from the region of Medina and the tribe left with their wealth packed on their camels, some heading north to the town of Khaybar, others going on further to Syria. Some of the Medinan Muslims protested the punishment of exile, saying to the Prophet: "Our sons and brothers are among them!"[32] Indeed, some of the children of the Medinans had been raised within the Jewish faith and were living with their adopted clan. In response to the dissatisfaction of the Medinan Muslims the words of the Qur'ān were revealed: *There is no compulsion in religion, for truth has been made clear from error*, meaning essentially that these "sons and brothers" had made their choice to stay loyal to a treacherous group against the Prophet, as well as against their own Muslim relatives, and were party to a plan to murder God's messenger. In this way, the words of verse 2:256, although harsh from a certain point of view, also reveal an essential principle within the Muslim faith: no one can be compelled to accept a religion, be it Islam

[30] Al-Ṭabarī, *Jāmi' al-bayān*, vol. 3, p. 21; Ibn Kathīr, *Tafsīr*, vol. 1, p. 417.

[31] We shall speak of this alliance known as the Constitution of Medina later in this essay.

[32] Al-Ṭabarī, *Jāmi' al-bayān*, vol. 3, p. 22. See also Wāḥidī, *Asbāb al-nuzūl* (Beirut: 'Ālam al-Kutub, 1970), p. 58 and Abū Dāwūd, *Sunan*, vol. 2, pp. 262–263 (*Kitāb al-jihad*, ḥadīth n. 2682).

or any other faith. This particular narration of the context of 2:256 is highly significant for delineating the attitude of Muslims on this issue, occurring as it does during the jihad of the siege of the Banū Naḍīr and rejecting, within that context, any compulsion in religion.

Another variant on this same story speaks of the people of Medina desiring to compel those of their "sons and brothers" affiliated with another Jewish tribe in the city, the Banū Qurayẓah, into accepting Islam. This version (whose number of narrations in the sources is much fewer than that of the Banū Naḍīr narrations) makes no mention of there being any hostilities at that time between the Muslims and the Jews, but only recounts the desire of the Medinan Muslims to force their Jewish relatives into Islam. In these narrations the Prophet responds to their desire to compel their family members with the words of 2:256,[33] again affirming the absolute necessity of freedom in choosing one's faith. This principle is also brought out in relation to a third possible context for the revelation of verse 2:256. This is said to be the conversion to Christianity of the sons of Abū'l-Ḥusayn a companion of the Prophet. The story is told that the two sons of Abū'l-Ḥusayn were converted in Medina by Christian merchants visiting the city from Syria. They then returned to Syria with the merchants.[34] Upon hearing of what his sons had done, Abū'l-Ḥusayn went to the Prophet and asked for permission to pursue them and bring them back. The Prophet then recited to him, "There is no compulsion in religion [...]." After Abū'l-Ḥusayn heard the words of the revelation, the narration concludes, "So he let them go their way".[35]

[33] See al-Ṭabarī, *Jāmi 'al-bayān*, vol. 3, p. 23.

[34] Al-Ṭabarī, *Jāmi' al-bayān*, vol. 3, p. 220; Ibn Kathīr, *Tafsīr*, vol. 1, p. 417; Wāḥidī, *Asbāb al-nuzūl*, pp. 58–59.

[35] It should also be noted that in the case of one version of this story (see al-Ṭabarī, *Jāmi' al-bayān*, vol. 3, p. 22 and Wāḥidī, *Asbāb al-nuzūl*, pp. 58–59), the Prophet, after pronouncing the Qur'ānic verse, then says, "God banish them! They are the first ones to disbelieve". This statement requires some explanation and needs to be understood in the context of the time. It can be said from the Islamic point of view that the actions of Abū'l-Ḥuṣayn's sons represent a grave error, because they were rejecting a prophet within his own lifetime, a prophet whom they knew personally. The actions of Abū'l-Ḥuṣayn's sons represent a denial of the immediate presence of the truth, and this is very different than, for instance, someone choosing not to accept the message of Islam today; one who never had the chance to actually see the Prophet Muhammad ﷺ, who was the living embodiment of submission to God. Like the words of Christ, "He who has seen me has seen the truth", the Prophet said, "He who has seen me has seen his Lord", thereby placing great responsibility on the shoulders of those who were privileged to encounter him. The strident words of the Prophet about the sons of Abū'l-Ḥuṣayn need to be understood in this context.

Regardless of the version of the story that we examine, the message is always the same—to choose one's own religion is a free choice whether in time of peace or war. Ibn Kathīr's commentary upon 2:256 also reflects this fact when he says:

> God, the Exalted, said, "There is no compulsion in religion," that is to say, you do not compel anyone to enter the religion of Islam. Truly it is made clear [and] evident. It [Islam] is not in need such that one compel anyone to enter it. Rather, the one whom God guides to Islam and expands his breast and illuminates his vision, he enters into it by way of clear proof. It is of no use to enter the religion as one compelled by force.[36]

Although these words are hardly ambiguous, we should also note that there have been those in the Islamic tradition who have tried to say that this Qur'ānic verse was later abrogated, but this is not the opinion of either of our commentators. Both al-Ṭabarī and Ibn Kathīr note that 2:256 has never been abrogated by any other verse(s) of the Qur'ān and that although 2:256 descended in regard to a particular case (*khaṣṣ*), i.e., in regard to either the Jews of Medina or the Christians from Syria, nevertheless, its application is general (*'amm*).[37] This is to say, the verse applies to all People of the Book, who should be free from being compelled to accept Islam.[38]

[36] Ibn Kathīr, *Tafsīr*, vol. 1, p. 416.

[37] Al-Ṭabarī, *Jāmi' al-bayān*, vol. 3, p. 25; Ibn Kathīr, *Tafsīr*, vol. 1, p. 417.

[38] Moreover this injunction is reflected elsewhere in the Qur'ān, such as in the verse, *For each we have given a law and a way, and had God willed He could have made you one people, but that He might put you to the test in what He has given you* [He has made you as you are]. *So vie with one another in good works. To God will you all be brought back, and He will inform you about that wherein you differed.* (Qur'ān 5:48) The universality and indeed acceptance of other "ways" and "laws" evident in this verse is to be seen even more directly in verse 2:62: "Those who say 'We are Jews' and 'We are Christians' and 'We are Sabians', all who believe in God and the Last Day and do good works, they have their reward with their Lord and neither shall they fear nor grieve." The word "Sabians" may be a reference to the remnants of a group of followers of St. John the Baptist, but in any case the message of this verse is very far from the fallacious notion that Islam denies the truth of other faiths. Indeed, the Qur'ān demands that Jews and Christians judge according to what God has given them in the Torah and the Gospel. This is evident in the Qur'ānic statement, *Truly, We revealed the Torah. In it is a guidance and light. By it the prophets who submitted* [to God] *judged the Jews* [...] *with what they were entrusted of the Book of God, and they were witnesses to it. Therefore, fear not men, but fear Me. Sell not My signs for little gain. Whoever does not judge by that which God has revealed, those are the unbelievers. We ordained therein* [within the Torah]*: a life for a life, an eye for an eye, nose for a nose, an ear for an ear, a tooth for a tooth, and wounds for retaliation. But if any one remits it then it is a penance for him, and whosoever does not judge by that which God has revealed, they are wrongdoers.* (Qur'ān 5:44–45) In relation to the followers of the Gospel, the Qur'ān says, *We sent him* [Jesus] *the Gospel. Therein is a guidance and a light* [...]. *Let the People of the Gospel judge by that which God*

"HAD GOD NOT REPELLED SOME MEN BY MEANS OF OTHERS [...]"

A related issue which goes beyond the simple idea of not forcing anyone into Islam is the fact that one of the essential and expressed elements of the earliest military jihad was the protection of the rights of worship of the People of the Book, i.e., not simply avoiding using force to bring them into Islam, but actively using force to preserve and defend their houses of worship. This characteristic of the military jihad is mentioned in verses 22:39–40 and, as we shall see, it is confirmed by many historical examples.

We noted earlier that verses 2:190–191 are sometimes claimed to be the first verses revealed relating to military jihad. This claim is also made for verses 22:39–40.[39] It is, of course, impossible to determine on the basis of the narrations given in the sources which group of verses is truly the first to speak of military jihad, but the Islamic tradition in general has simply accepted ambiguity on this issue. Verses 22:39–40 say:

> *Permission is given to those who are fought because they have been wronged. Surely, God is able to give them victory,*
>
> *Those who have been expelled from their homes unjustly only because they said: "Our Lord is God." And if it were not that God repelled some people by means of others, then monasteries, churches, synagogues, and mosques, wherein the Name of God is mentioned much would surely have been pulled down. Verily, God will help those who help Him. Truly, God is powerful and mighty.*

Our commentators tell us that these verses were revealed just as the Prophet Muhammad ﷺ and his companions were leaving Makka and migrating to Medina.[40] Both al-Ṭabarī and Ibn Kathīr relay the words of Abū Bakr al-Ṣiddīq upon hearing the new revelation. He is reported to have said, "I knew [when I heard it] that it would be fighting (*qitāl*) [between the Muslims and the Makkans]".[41] It is also interesting to note that al-Ṭabarī

has revealed therein. Whosoever does not judge by that which God has revealed, those are the corrupt. (Qur'ān 5: 46–47) Therefore, not only are the People of the Torah and of the Gospel not to be compelled to accept Islam, but they must, according to the Qur'ān, be free to make their own decisions based upon what their scriptures reveal to them. Moreover, for them not to do so is displeasing to God.

39 Al-Ṭabarī, *Jāmi' al-bayān*, vol. 10, p. 227–228; Ibn Kathīr, *Tafsīr*, vol. 3, p. 303.

40 Al-Ṭabarī, *Jāmi' al-bayān*, vol. 10, p. 226; Ibn Kathīr, *Tafsīr*, vol. 3, p. 302.

41 Al-Ṭabarī, *Jāmi' al-bayān*, vol. 10, p. 227; Ibn Kathīr, *Tafsīr*, vol. 3, p. 303.

relates traditions that state that the meaning of the phrase "if it were not that God repelled some people by means of others" is "if it were not for fighting and jihad" and "if it were not for fighting and jihad in the way of God".[42] Furthermore, Ibn Kathīr relates that many famous early figures of Islam "such as Ibn 'Abbās, Mujāhid, 'Urwah ibn al-Zubayr, Zayd ibn Aslam, Muqātil ibn Ḥayyān, Qatādah and others" also said that "this is the first verse revealed concerning jihad".[43] These commentaries are particularly important because all of them refer to the fact that jihad is to be understood, in its earliest sense, as a means by which "monasteries, churches, synagogues, and mosques" are to be preserved and protected.[44] The call to jihad then was not for the destruction of faiths other than Islam; rather, one of its essential aspects was the preservation of places of worship belonging to the monotheistic faiths and protecting them against those polytheists—in this case the idolaters of Makka—who might endanger them.

SOME APPLICATIONS OF QUR'ĀNIC PRINCIPLES TO THE MILITARY JIHAD

When we turn to the many examples of the early military jihad found in the sources, we see that the Muslim armies were actually quite consistent in their application of the Qur'ānic doctrines mentioned in 22:39–40 and 2:256. Although the historical record does not speak definitively about the issue of whether or not these endeavours were strictly defensive—for as with all such undertakings, they involved both elements of true religious fervour and righteousness, as well as issues of the *realpolitik* of the time—what can be said rather definitively is that the Muslim forces, in carrying out the early jihad, did act in accordance with the limits established by the

[42] Al-Ṭabarī *Jāmi' al-bayān*, vol. 10, p. 229.

[43] Ibn Kathīr, *Tafsīr*, vol. 3, p. 303.

[44] Maḥmūd Shaltūt (d. 1963), the former Shaykh al-Azhar, arguably the most important exoteric authority in the Islamic world, commented upon these verses in his book *al-Qur'ān wa'l-qitāl* (*The Qur'an and Fighting*, trans. Peters [in *Jihad*, p. 43]) as follows: "These verses are, as we have said, the first verses of fighting. They are clear and do not contain even the slightest evidence of religious compulsion. On the contrary, they confirm that the practice that the people ward off each other is one of God's principles in creation, inevitable for the preservation of order and for the continuation of righteousness and civilization. Were it not for this principle, the earth would have been ruined and all different places of worship would have been destroyed. This would have happened if powerful tyrants would have held sway over religions, free to abuse them without restraint and to force people to conversion, without anyone to interfere. These verses are not only concerned with Muslims, but have clearly a general impact [...]."

Qur'ān and ḥadīth. We know this from the examination of the accounts presented in the various Islamic histories, such as al-Ṭabarī's universal history, *Ta'rīkh al-rusūl wa'l-mulūk*, as well as other important historical works that specialise in the events of the early jihad, such as Balādhurī's (d. 279 AH/892 CE) *Futūḥ al-buldān* or "Openings of the Nations". In these accounts, there is clear evidence of the importance Muslims attached to the idea of "no compulsion in religion", as well as to the preservation of the places of worship of the People of the Book. Balādhurī, for instance, recounts a text written by the Prophet to the Christian community of Najrān in southern Arabia guaranteeing them certain social and religious rights under Islamic rule. The text reads:

> Najrān and their followers are entitled to the protection of Allāh and to the security of Muhammad the Prophet, the Messenger of Allāh, which security shall involve their persons, religion, lands, and possessions, including those of them who are absent as well as those who are present, their camels, messengers, and images [*amthila*, a reference to crosses and icons]. The state they previously held shall not be changed, nor shall any of their religious services or images be changed. No attempt shall be made to turn a bishop, a monk from his office as a monk, nor the sexton of a church from his office.[45]

Both al-Ṭabarī and Balādhurī make many references to similar treaties concluded between Muslim commanders during the early jihad effort and the various populations that fell under Islamic political control. Indeed, such examples are to be found on every major front of the Islamic conquests from Persia to Egypt and all areas in between. Within the region of Syria, we have the example of the companion of the Prophet and commander of Muslim forces Abū 'Ubaydah ibn al-Jarrāḥ, who concluded an agreement with the Christian population of Aleppo granting them safety for "their lives, their possessions, city wall, churches, homes, and the fort". Abū 'Ubaydah is said to have concluded similar treaties at Antioch,[46] Ma'arrat Maṣrīn,[47] Ḥimṣ,[48] Qinnasrīn,[49] and Ba'labakk.[50] Balādhurī reports

[45] Balādhurī, *Origins*, vol. 1, p. 100.
[46] Ibid., vol. 1, p. 227.
[47] Ibid., vol. 1, p. 229.
[48] Ibid., vol. 1, p. 187.
[49] Ibid., vol. 1, p. 223.
[50] Ibid., vol. 1, pp. 198–199.

that after the surrender of Damascus, Khālid ibn al-Walīd wrote for the inhabitants of the city a document stating:

> In the Name of Allāh, the compassionate, the merciful. This is what Khālid would grant to the inhabitants of Damascus, if he enters therein: he promises to give them security for their lives, property, and churches. Their city shall not be demolished; neither shall any Moslem be quartered in their houses. Thereunto we give to them the pact of Allāh and the protection of his Prophet, the caliphs and the "Believers". So long as they pay the poll-tax,[51] nothing but good shall befall them.[52]

In addition to these accounts, al-Ṭabarī records the "Covenant of 'Umar", a document apparently addressed to the people of the city of Jerusalem, which was conquered in the year 636 CE/15 AH. The document states:

> This is the assurance of safety (*aman*) which the servant of God 'Umar, the Commander of the Faithful, has granted to the people of Jerusalem. He has given them an assurance of safety for themselves, for their property, their churches, their crosses, the sick and the healthy of the city, and for all the rituals that belong to their religion. Their churches will not be inhabited [by Muslims] and will not be destroyed. Neither they, nor the land on which they stand, nor their crosses, nor their property will be damaged. They will not be forcibly converted [...] The people of Jerusalem must pay the poll tax like the people of [other] cities, and they must expel the Byzantines and the robbers [...].[53]

[51] The poll-tax or jizya was required to be paid by the People of the Book to the Islamic state according to verse 9:29 of the Qur'ān and certain ḥadīth. This tax, unlike feudal taxation in Europe, did not constitute an economic hardship for non-Muslims living under Muslim rule. The tax was seen as the legitimate right of the Islamic state, given that all peoples—Muslim and non-Muslim—benefited from the military protection of the state, the freedom of the roads, and trade, etc. Although the jizya was paid by non-Muslims, Muslims were also taxed through the *zakāt*, a required religious tax not levied on other communities.

[52] Balādhurī, *Origins*, vol. 1, p. 187.

[53] Al-Ṭabarī, *The History of al-Ṭabarī, v. XII: The Battle of al-Qādisiyya and the Conquest of Syria and Palestine*, trans. Y. Friedmann (Albany: SUNY Press, 1985), p. 191. The useof the word "Byzantines" here should not be conflated with "Christians". "Byzantines" refers to those people who were the administrators of Byzantine authority in the lands that were now conquered by the Muslims. The very fact that the word "Byzantines" is used, and not "Christians" is significant. This shows that it was not "Christianity" but rather the political and military opposition of Byzantium that was at issue. It was because of this opposition that the Byzantines needed to be expelled. Byzantine administrators and

These conditions, respecting Christian practices and places of worship, were also given to other towns throughout Palestine, according to al-Ṭabarī.[54] In regard to the Armenian front, we have references to treaties made with Jewish and Christian as well as Zoroastrian inhabitants of the region. It is noteworthy that both al-Ṭabarī and Ibn Kathīr in their Qur'ān commentaries mention Zoroastrians (*al-majūs*) within the classification of "People of the Book"[55]—Zoroastrianism being the other major faith, besides Judaism and Christianity, that was encountered by the Muslim armies as they spread out of Arabia and which, like Judaism and Christianity, possessed a sacred text. Balādhurī mentions the treaty concluded by the Companion of the Prophet, Ḥabīb ibn Maslamah al-Fihrī (d. 662 CE/42 AH), with the people of the town of Dabīl which states:

> In the name of Allāh, the compassionate, the merciful. This is a treaty of Ḥabīb ibn Maslamah with the Christians, Magians [i.e., Zoroastrians], and Jews of Dabīl, including those present and absent. I have granted for you safety for your lives, possessions, churches, places of worship, and city wall. Thus ye are safe and we are bound to fulfill our covenant, so long as ye fulfill yours and pay the poll-tax [...].[56]

In addition to this, al-Ṭabarī mentions treaties that the Muslims made with the Armenians of al-Bāb and Mūqān in the Caucasus Mountains guaranteeing "their possessions, their persons, [and] their religion".[57]

When we turn to the region of Persia, Balādhurī mentions two agreements, one with the people of Rayy,[58] and the other with the people

officials, like the "robbers" also mentioned in the quotation, were a possible source of social unrest and political chaos. Just as there cannot be two kings ruling a single kingdom, the Muslims needed to remove any vestiges of Byzantine political authority in the lands they now controlled. This did not mean the removal of the vestiges of "Christianity" from those lands, for the quotation itself also mentions preserving the rights of Christians to practice their faith and maintain their churches, crosses, etc., under the new Islamic government.

[54] Ibid., pp. 191–192. Al-Ṭabarī indicates that similar letters were written to "all the provinces" around Jerusalem as well as to the "people of Lydda and all the people of Palestine".

[55] Al-Ṭabarī, *Jāmi 'al-bayān*, vol. 3, pp. 24–25; Ibn Kathīr, *Tafsīr*, vol. 2, pp. 457–458. This position has been generally agreed upon by most of the early scholars of Islamic law; see for instance the comments of Ibn Rushd in his *Bidāyat al-mujtahid*, in Peters, *Jihad*, p. 24.

[56] Balādhurī, *Origins*, vol. 1, p. 314.

[57] Al-Ṭabarī, *The History of al-Ṭabarī, v. XIV: The Conquest of Iran*, trans. G. Rex Smith (Albany: SUNY Press, 1994), pp. 36–38.

[58] Balādhurī, *Origins*, vol. 2, p. 4.

of Ādhārbayjān.[59] The texts of each of these agreements guarantees the safety of the lives of the inhabitants, as well as offering a promise not to "raze any of their fire temples", a reference to Zoroastrian *ātashkādas*. In al-Ṭabarī's *history* as well, treaties are recounted involving the town of Qūmis,[60] the peoples of Dihistān in the province of Jurjān,[61] and the people of Ādhārbayjān,[62] each treaty granting "safety […] for their religion". Finally, in Egypt we can point to the example of 'Amr ibn al-'Āṣ, a companion of the Prophet and the commander of Muslim forces on the Egyptian front. He concluded a treaty with the Bishop of Alexandria on the orders of the Caliph 'Umar, guaranteeing the safety of the city and agreeing to return certain Christian captives taken by the Muslims after an initial skirmish. According to al-Ṭabarī, 'Umar's instructions to 'Amr were as follows:

> […] propose to the ruler of Alexandria that he give you the *jizya* in the understanding that those of their people who were taken prisoner and who are still in your care be offered the choice between Islam and the religion of their own people. Should any one of them opt for Islam, then he belongs to the Muslims, with the same privileges and obligations as they. And he who opts for the religion of his own people has to pay the same jizya as will be imposed on his co-religionists.[63]

'Amr also concluded an agreement with Abū Maryam, the Metropolitan of Miṣr. Al-Ṭabarī quotes 'Amr's words in an apparent face to face meeting with the Metropolitan:

> We call upon you to embrace Islam. He who is willing to do so will be like one of us. To him who refuses, we suggest that he pay the jizya and we will give him ample protection. Our Prophet […] has determined that we keep you from harm […]. If you accept our proposition, we will give you constant protection.[64]

[59] Ibid., p. 20.

[60] Al-Ṭabarī, *The History of al-Ṭabarī, v. XIV: The Conquest of Iran*, p. 28.

[61] Ibid., p. 29.

[62] Ibid., p. 33.

[63] Al-Ṭabarī, *The History of al-Ṭabarī, v. XIII: The Conquest of Iraq, Southwestern Persia, and Egypt*, trans. G. Ḥ A. Juynboll (Albany: SUNY Press, 1985), pp. 164–165.

[64] Ibid., pp. 167–168.

Al-Ṭabarī then quotes the actual text of the treaty agreed to between them as follows:

> In the name of God, the merciful, the compassionate.
>
> This is the text of the covenant that 'Amr b. al-'Āṣ has granted the people of Miṣr concerning immunity for themselves, their religion, their possessions, churches, crucifixes, as well as their land and their waterways [...]. It is incumbent upon the people of Miṣr, if they agree on the terms of this covenant and when the rise of the Nile water comes to a halt to afford the jizya [...]. He who chooses [not to agree to these terms but] to depart will enjoy immunity, until he has reached his destination where he can be safe, or has moved out of the territory where our authority prevails.[65]

With these treaties in mind we can now return to a question which we raised earlier: Who, in the opinion of the early Muslims, were the People of the Book that had to be fought? In short, given this picture of the history, the answer to this question is that those who were to be fought among the People of the Book were only those who refused to submit to Islamic political authority, i.e., who refused to pay the poll-tax (jizya). The Muslims made no hair-splitting theological determinations regarding the issue of "true belief", as some might think is implied in certain Qur'ānic verses that we quoted earlier. All People of the Book were simply treated as "believers" within their respective religious communities, regardless of whether they followed, for instance, in the case of Christianity, a Monophysite, Arian, Jacobite, Nestorian, or Catholic rite. There was no litmus test of faith which the Muslims applied to determine true belief on the part of the people who came under their political control, other than the self-declarations of those people themselves to be Jews, Christians, or Zoroastrians, and their willingness to pay the jizya.[66] The earliest mujāhidūn, the Prophet, his companions, and their immediate successors, essentially placed all People of the Book under the general category of "faith". This fact played itself out not only in terms of treaties concluded between Muslims and non-Muslims, which as we have seen demonstrate no theological scrutiny of non-Muslim

[65] Ibid., pp. 170–171.

[66] The issue as to whether the Muslims may accept the jizya from the mushrikūn or polytheists, thereby granting them protected (*dhimmī*) status under the Islamic state, like the status of the People of the Book, has been debated by scholars of Islamic law. For various opinions on this issue see Ibn Rushd, *Bidāyat al-mujtahid*, in Peters, *Jihad*, pp. 24–25.

communities, but also in terms of the very composition of the "Muslim" forces involved in the jihad, to which we will now turn.

THE COMPOSITION OF THE FORCES OF JIHAD

In relation to the practice of the military jihad we can see that Islam's universal perspective on faith also had an important effect on the make-up of the "Muslim" armies. Here we can point to the fact that military jihad was not seen as the exclusive prerogative of Muslims. This is particularly true during the formative years of the Islamic conquests, i.e., from the first command to military jihad in Medina through the early Umayyad period. Again, this is made clear in various treaties that the Muslims concluded with both the Jewish and Christian populations of the Near East at this time. Perhaps the most famous of these treaties is the Constitution of Medina, which was composed during the lifetime of the Prophet himself and which speaks of the Jews and Muslims fighting together as one umma or community.

THE CONSTITUTION OF MEDINA

The Constitution of Medina, recorded in Ibn Isḥāq's (d. 768 CE/151 AH) *Sīrāṭ Rasūl Allāh* (*The Biography of the Messenger of God*), the most important historical account of the life of the Prophet, indicates that jihad was for any community willing to fight alongside the Muslims (with the exceptions of polytheists). Ibn Isḥāq prefaces his account of the Constitution by saying:

> The Messenger of God (God bless and preserve him) wrote a writing between the Emigrants and the *Anṣār*,[67] in which he made a treaty and covenant with the Jews, confirmed their religion and possessions, and gave them certain rights and duties.[68]

[67] These terms may need some explanation. The people of the city of Makka were almost all members of an Arabic tribe known as Quraysh, and the Prophet and the vast majority of his early followers in Makka were also members of this tribe. When the Prophet left Makka for the city of Medina, an event known as the *hijra* or migration, those members of his community who journeyed with him were given the title of muhājirūn or "Emigrants". As for the term *anṣār*, it refers to those people of Medina who accepted the Islamic message and invited the Prophet and the Emigrants to the city, giving them refuge from their situation of persecution in Makka. For this reason these residents of Medina were given the title of *anṣār* or "Helpers", due to the fact that they gave safe haven to the Prophet and the Emigrants.

[68] W. M. Watt, *Muhammad at Medina* (Oxford: Clarendon Press, 1956), p. 221.

The text of the treaty then follows:

> In the name of God, the Merciful, the Compassionate! This is a writing of Muhammad the prophet between the believers and Muslims of Quraysh and Yathrib[69] and those who follow them and are attached to them *and who crusade (jāhada) along with them*. They are a single community distinct from other people [...]. Whosoever of the Jews follows us has the (same) help and support [...], so long as they are not wronged [by him] and he does not help [others] against them.[70] [emphasis added]

Here we see that the participation in "military jihad", translated above as "crusade", is open to those "attached" to the Prophet and the Muslims, and that together they constitute a "single community" (*umma wāḥida*) in the face of all others. It is interesting to note that the claim that animosity has always existed between Muslims and Jews does not accord with this very early document dealing with military cooperation and mutual protection between the two communities.[71] Indeed the treaty seems not only to form a basis for an important military alliance between the Muslim and Jewish communities, but it also anticipates orderly and peaceful interactions on a general social level. Thus the Constitution goes on to say:

> The Jews bear expenses along with the believers so long as they continue at war. The Jews of Banū 'Awf are a community (umma) along with the believers. To the Jews their religion (*dīn*) and to the Muslims their religion. [This applies]

[69] The term "Yathrib" actually refers to the city of Medina. Before the time of Islam, Medina was called "Yathrib". The name "Medina" came to be used later as a result of the fact that the city was eventually renamed "Madīnat al-Nabī" (The City of the Prophet). Today the city is simply referred to by the first part of this title, Medina, or "The City".

[70] Watt, *Muhammad*, p. 221.

[71] It may be asked if this pact of mutual protection does not contradict the point made earlier concerning verse 5:51. We stated that 5:51 essentially tells the Muslims not to take Jews (or Christians) as their "protectors" in a military sense, and yet the Constitution seems to be doing just that by stating that between Muslims and Jews is "help against whoever wars against the people of this document." Is this not then taking Jews as "protectors"? In answer to this question it needs to be said that the specific context of 5:51 is that of individual Muslims taking alliances with those outside the umma in order to save their own individual lives and thereby endangering the unity and internal strength of the Muslims. It does not refer to a context in which the Muslims, as an umma, agree to a treaty for the benefit and safety of the umma as a whole. This issue points out the necessity of clearly understanding the *asbāb al-nuzūl* of Qur'ānic passages. Without such understanding a mistake could be made such that all agreements of help or assistance between Muslims and non-Muslims would be seen as compromising Islam; but this is simply not the context of 5:51. Indeed if it were, it would compromise practically the entire early history of the jihad effort which is filled with agreements of protection and assistance, as we see with the Constitution and as we shall see in other parts of this essay.

> both to their clients and to themselves, with the exception of anyone who has done wrong or acted treacherously; he brings evil only on himself and on his household. For the Jews of Banū 'n-Najjār the like of what is for the Jews of the Banū 'Awf. For the Jews of Banū'l-Ḥarith the like [...]. For the Jews of Banū Sa'īdah the like [...]. For the Jews of Banū Jusham the like [...]. For the Jews of Banū'l-Aws the like [...]. For the Jews of Banū Tha'labah the like of what is for the Jews of Banū 'Awf [...].[72]

Another portion of the document speaks more directly about the social attitudes that should form the basis of interaction:

> Between them [Muslims and Jews] there is help against whoever wars against the people of this document. Between them is sincere friendship and honorable dealing, not treachery. A man is not guilty of treachery through [the act of] his confederate. There is help for the person wronged.[73]

What this document shows is that early in the life of the Islamic community, there was the anticipation of normal and "friendly" relations between the Jews and Muslims and indeed, help between them in terms of war. These ideas are also supported by the authenticity generally accorded to the Constitution by modern scholarship. In terms of this authenticity, both the language and the content of the document suggest that it is an early piece of work, i.e., pre-Umayyad.[74] This is due to the fact that later falsifiers, writing during the time of the Umayyads or the 'Abbāsids, would not likely have included non-Muslims as members of the umma (a term later reserved for the Muslim community exclusively), nor retained the other articles of the document (from which we did not quote) that speak against the Quraysh,[75]

[72] Watt, *Muhammad*, p. 222.

[73] Ibid, p. 224.

[74] The Umayyad Dynasty ruled the Islamic world immediately following the end of the "Rightly-guided caliphate" (661 CE/40 AH) until they were overthrown by the 'Abbāsids in 750 CE/132 AH who established their own dynasty, which ruled over all Muslim lands (in a nominal way from the 10th century CE/4th century AH onward) until the Mongol conquest of their capital at Baghdad in the 13th century CE/7th century AE, at which time the last 'Abbāsids caliph was killed.

[75] Such comments criticizing the tribe of Quraysh would have been construed by the Umayyads (see note 67) as a critique of their legitimacy, given that the Umayyad's drew their legitimacy from their status as descendents of one of the prominent clans of Quraysh. The importance that they placed upon this Qurayshi lineage was as a result of the fact that, within the tribe of Quraysh, they were not descendents of the immediate clan of the Prophet, i.e., the clan of Hāshim, but of another clan within Quraysh, the clan of 'Abd Shams. Thus, it was not through their immediate clan but through their more distant Qurayshi heritage that they could claim a relation to the Prophetic substance of Muhammad.

nor made such prevalent and constant use of the term *mu'minūn* (believers) rather than *muslimūn* to refer to the followers of the Prophet and his message.[76] Both Julius Wellhausen and Leone Caetani placed the writing of the document sometime before the battle of Badr. Hubert Grimme argued for a date just after Badr, and W. Montgomery Watt, a date following siege of the Banū Qurayẓah (626 CE/5 AH).[77] In any case, it is clear that we are dealing here with a document whose early date of composition is claimed both from within and from without the tradition, suggesting a high degree of reliability that it does indeed express early Islamic attitudes toward the openness of the institution of military jihad.

CHRISTIANS IN JIHAD

Another important point regarding the armies of jihad is that traditional Islamic histories give accounts of Christians taking part in some of the early battles alongside the Muslim armies. This is discussed by Fred Donner in his book *The Early Islamic Conquests*. He notes that, according to Muslim historical sources, in the very early period of jihad, Christian Arabs from tribes such as the Banū Ṭayyi' of Najd, the Banū al-Namir ibn Qāsiṭ of the upper Euphrates river valley, and the Banū Lakhm participated in the jihad with the Muslim armies.[78] Other allusions to this kind of activity can be found in al-Ṭabarī's *Ta'rīkh* where he notes, for instance, a treaty signed during the reign of the caliph 'Umar by Surāqah ibn 'Amr in 646 CE/22 AH. Surāqah was a commander of Muslim forces in Armenia, which was predominantly Christian. The treaty discusses the poll-tax which the Christian population is to pay to the Islamic government, unless they are willing to supply soldiers to the jihad effort, in which case the poll-tax would be

[76] Although the Qur'ān discusses both mu'minūn and muslimūn in referring to those who followed the message of the Prophet Muhammad ﷺ, most early theological and sectarian documents refer to members of the Islamic community as mu'minūn or "believers", rather than muslimūn specifically. For example, the early sectarian writings of the Khārijites and Murji'ites always discussed issues of membership in the Islamic community in terms of "believers" and non-believers, not in terms of Muslims and non-Muslims.

[77] Watt, *Muhammad*, pp. 225–227.

[78] Fred M. Donner, *The Early Islamic Conquests* (Princeton: Princeton University Press, 1981), p. 200.

cancelled.[79] In addition to this account, Balādhurī notes many other agreements in the *Futūḥ al-buldān* concluded by Muslim commanders with the Christian populations of various regions. Such is the case of the Jarājimah, a Christian people from the town of Jurjāmah.[80] This town had been under the control of the patrician and governor of Antioch but surrendered to the Muslim armies, commanded by Ḥabīb ibn Maslamah al-Fihrī, when they attacked the town. Balādhurī recounts the terms of the peace between Ḥabīb and the Jarājimah as follows:

> Terms were made providing that al-Jarājimah would act as helpers to the Moslems, and as spies and frontier garrison in Mount al-Lukam. On the other hand it was stipulated that they pay no tax, and that they keep for themselves the booty they take from the enemy in case they fight with the Moslems.[81]

Here jihad is an endeavor open to the Christian Jarājimah. Another treaty concluded with them during the reign of the Umayyad Caliph al-Walīd ibn 'Abd al-Malik (705–715 CE/86–96 AH), states:

> Al-Jarājimah may settle wherever they wish in Syria [...]; neither they nor any of their children or women should be compelled to leave Christianity; they may put on Moslem dress; and no poll-tax may be assessed on them, their children, or women. On the other hand, they should take part in the Moslem campaigns and be allowed to keep for themselves the booty from those whom they kill [...]; and the same amount taken from the possessions of the Moslems should be taken [as tax] from their articles of trade and the possessions of the wealthy among them.[82]

[79] Al-Ṭabarī, *The History of al-Ṭabarī, v. XIV*, p. 36. The text of the treaty is:

In the name of God, the Compassionate, the Merciful. This is the safe-conduct Surāqah b. 'Amr, governor of the Commander of the Faithful, 'Umar b. al-Khaṭṭāb, has granted to Shahrbarāz, the inhabitants of Armenia, and the Armenians [in al-Bāb]. [He grants] them safe-conduct for their persons, their possessions, and their religion lest they be harmed and so that nothing be taken from them. [The following is imposed] upon the people of Armenia and al-Abwāb, those coming from distant parts and those who are local and those around them who have joined them: that they should participate in any military expedition, and carry out any task, actual or potential, that the governor considers to be for the good, providing that those who agree to this are exempt from tribute but [perform] military service. Military service shall be instead of their paying tribute. But those of them who are not needed for military service and who remain inactive have similar tribute obligations to the people of Azerbaijan [in general] [...]. If they perform military service, they are exempt from [all] this.

[80] Jurjūmah was located in the border region between modern-day Syria and Turkey.

[81] Balādhurī, *Origins*, vol. 1, p. 246.

[82] Ibid., p. 249.

These agreements, along with the many others that we have noted in the previous sections, in addition to revealing something of the martial applications of Islam's universal perspective on faith, also demonstrate that historically jihad was directed against those who stood in opposition to the political authority of the Islamic state. It was not directed against a people simply because they professed a faith other than Islam. The point of the jihad was not to establish a world populated only by Muslims; it was to create a social order in which the freedom to practice the worship of God was guaranteed, for Muslims as well as for the People of the Book. Although military jihad had as its goal the establishment of this Islamic authority, there were also certain essential and religiously unavoidable limitations placed upon the means to achieving this goal. These limitations were defined by the injunctions of the Qur'ān and the ḥadīth and manifested, as well as clarified, by the conduct of the earliest mujāhidūn, the Prophet, and his companions. These teachings and examples have served as an indispensable guide to Muslims throughout their 1400-year history, not only in terms of jihad but in relation to all matters of faith. When we look at the attempts of certain contemporary figures to revive the military jihad, their words and actions must always be judged by way of the limits and examples mentioned in the early tradition. This is the only way to determine the essential "Islamicity" of their claims and to know if their actions constitute some form of reprehensible (*makrūh*) or forbidden (*ḥarām*) innovation (*bid'a*) upon the tradition.[83] Muslims have always been cautioned to exercise the utmost care when introducing new interpretations or practices, as a famous ḥadīth of the Prophet states: "Beware of newly invented matters, for every invented matter is an innovation, every innovation is a going astray, and every going astray is in Hell-fire".[84]

[83] For a full explanation of the traditional Islamic teachings on innovation (*bid'a*) see Ṭ J. Winter's "The Poverty of Fanaticism" in Joseph E. B. Lumbard ed., *Islam, Fundamentalism, and the Betrayal of Tradition* (World Wisdom Books, 2004).

[84] Al-Nawawī, *An-Nawawī's Forty Ḥadīth*, trans. by E. Ibrahim and D. Johnson Davies (Malaysia: Polygraphic Press Sdn. Bhd., 1982), p. 94 (ḥadīth 28). This ḥadīth is also to be found in the *Sunan* of Abū Dāwūd and the *Jāmi'* of Tirmidhī. Other ḥadīth related by al-Nawawī concerning the issue of innovation are: "He who establishes something in this matter of ours that is not from it, it is rejected (*radd*)!" and "The one who acts [in a way that is] not in agreement with our matter, it is rejected!"

SOME CONTEMPORARY FUNDAMENTALIST INTERPRETATIONS OF JIHAD

To begin our analysis it is perhaps best to start with the form of the jihad envisaged by the modern fundamentalists; that is to say, is the form of this jihad consistent with the established principles of the Islamic faith or not? It has been claimed that the jihad which Muslims must now wage involves "killing Americans and their allies—civilian and military". Any such declaration would immediately place the endeavor outside the bounds of true jihad whose limits, as we noted earlier, would clearly exclude, for instance, attacks upon women and children. In fact, the categories of "civilian" and "military" often used by these extremists are somewhat alien to the Islamic tradition which always speaks on this issue of warfare in terms of "those who fight against the Muslims" and "those who do not", the tradition being unanimous in defining "those who do not" as women and children, with other categories often times included such as monks and the elderly. Therefore, the declarations making "lawful" the indiscriminate killing of civilians unequivocally transgress the limits of warfare defined in the traditional sources. Indeed, some claim that now is the time for a new *fiqh* or jurisprudence in Islam that would leave behind such traditional constraints.[85] Some have even attempted to cast their arguments in the guise of religion by calling their declarations of jihad "fatwas"[86] and by quoting liberally from the Qur'ān. Of course, the determination of the "Islamicity" of any fatwa must be in relation to its content, and yet if we

[85] We should not have the impression that modern fundamentalists represent the first time that the traditional Islamic limits of warfare have been disregarded. The Khārijite movement, whose roots go back to a religio-political dispute in the first Islamic century, represent one of the most famous examples of just such transgression. The Khārijites were perfectly willing to attack "civilians", although their dispute was essentially with other members of the Muslim community rather than with non-Muslims. They declared a sentence of "excommunication" (*barā'a*) upon anyone who did not accept their perspective on Islam. According to the Khārijites, such excommunicated people—men, women, and children—were afforded no protection under the laws of religion for their lives or property. Therefore, the Khārijites considered it perfectly legal to kill such persons. It is important to mention that throughout the early history of Islam the Khārijite position was condemned and even physically opposed by every major Muslim group, Sunnī and Shī'ite.

[86] The choice of this word is a calculated political maneuver to co-opt the authority of the 1400-year Islamic legal tradition. Within the science of Islamic jurisprudence (*fiqh*), a fatwa refers to a religious opinion issued by a scholar of law (*sharī'a*). Most fundamentalists have had no formal training in the study of Islamic law.

analyse the Qur'ānic verses chosen by extremists to justify their own exegesis reveals that, far from being representatives of traditional Islam and the "pious forefathers" (*salaf*) of the Muslim community, their perspective is actually what we might call the "other side of the coin" of modernism, due to its near total disregard for the established contexts of the verses they quote.[87]

One verse often mentioned in this regard is verse 9:5: *But when the forbidden months are past, then fight and slay the polytheists* [mushrikūn] *wherever you find them, seize them, beleaguer them, and lie in wait for them in every stratagem* [of war]. It is interesting that this verse should be cited in the context of calls for Muslims to fight Jews and Christians, particularly since this verse has nothing to do with the issue of the People of the Book. As we mentioned earlier, the Qur'ān does not refer to Jews and Christians as mushrikūn but reserves this term for the idolatrous Arabs present at the time of the Prophet Muhammad ﷺ. In the case of verse 9:5, however, we are not dealing with a reference to the idolaters of Makka specifically because, according to tradition, the ninth chapter of the Qur'ān was revealed after the conquest of Makka by the Muslims, that is to say, at a time when there were no longer any polytheists in the city as a result of conversion to Islam. The mushrikūn referred to in verse 9:5 are therefore the Arab polytheists/idolaters who remained in other parts of Arabia not yet under Muslim control. This being the case, the use of 9:5 would represent a misappropriation of this verse to an end other than the one intended from its established traditional context of fighting the "pagan" Arabs.

Other verses which have become popular proof texts for the jihadist position are 9:36 and 2:193. The verses are, respectively: *And fight the polytheists* [mushrikūn] *together as they fight you together,*" and *Fight them* [i.e., the mushrikūn] *until there is no more oppression and religion is for God.* These verses have been cited as direct support for killing civilians, yet both these verses, as with verse 9:5, refer directly to fighting the mushrikūn, not Jews or Christians and certainly not civilians. Neither al-Ṭabarī nor Ibn Kathīr have much to say regarding 9:36, except to emphasize that the

[87] For an examination of the relationship between modernism and fundamentalism, see Joseph E. B. Lumbard's "The Decline of Knowledge and the Rise of Ideology in the Modern Islamic World", in Joseph E. B. Lumbard ed., *Islam, Fundamentalism, and the Betrayal of Tradition* (World Wisdom Books, 2004).

Muslims should act together or in unison during warfare against the polytheists. The injunction to "fight the polytheists together as they fight you together", which has sometimes been taken to mean that Muslims should respond in kind to the attacks of an enemy, cannot be understood as an invitation to transgress the established Islamic rules of warfare. It is telling in this regard that al-Ṭabarī and Ibn Kathīr only refer in their comments on 9:36 to the verse's meaning in relation to the "unity" of the umma, and do not mention issues of responding in kind to offenses, which would seem to be a subject worthy of at least some comment, if indeed that was the verse's intended meaning.

In terms of verse 2:193, Ibn Kathīr sees it as part of a series of related verses beginning with 2:190. Like al-Ṭabarī, he mentions that these verses refer to the first military jihad against the mushrikūn of Makka, and he also emphasises the fact that these verses are in no way an invitation to kill non-combatants, even those who live among the communities of the enemies of Islam. Like al-Ṭabarī, Ibn Kathīr in his comments quotes many narrations about the "transgressing of limits" in warfare, such as the words of the famous Qur'ān commentator and theologian Ḥasan al-Baṣrī (d. 728 CE), who said that the acts which transgress the limits of war are:

> [...] mutilation, [imposing] thirst, the killing of women, children, and the old—the ones who have no judgment for themselves, and no fighters are among them, [the killing of] monks and hermits, the burning of trees, and the killing animals for other than the welfare [of eating]".[88]

In addition to this, Ibn Kathīr mentions various sayings of the Prophet with meanings similar to the words of Ḥasan al-Baṣrī, such as:

> When he [the Prophet] dispatched his armies, he said, "Go in the name of God! Fight in the way of God [against] the ones who disbelieve in God! Do not act brutally![89] Do not exceed the proper bounds! Do not mutilate! Do not kill children or hermits!"[90]

As if such statements were not enough, from the Islamic point of view, to reject the indiscriminate violence endorsed by many fundamentalists,

[88] Ibn Kathīr, *Tafsīr*, vol. 1, p. 308.

[89] The command here in Arabic, *lā ta' ta dū*, means "not to act brutally", but it can also mean "not to commit excess, outrage, unlawful action, or violate women".

[90] Ibn Kathīr, *Tafsīr*, vol. 1, pp. 308–309.

Ibn Kathīr also relays another ḥadīth in which the Prophet Muhammad ﷺ tells the story of a community of people who were weak and poor and were being fought by a stronger group who showed animosity and harshness towards them. The Prophet says that the weaker group was eventually given help by God to overcome their enemies, but in their success, these weak ones became oppressors of those who had first tried to oppress them. He concludes with the words, "And God was displeased with them till the Day of Resurrection". The meaning of this prophetic story says Ibn Kathīr, is: "When they [the weak] possessed power over the strong, then they committed outrageous/unlawful/brutal acts against them [...] and God was displeased with them by reason of this brutality". Thus, Ibn Kathīr points out an important principle of warfare in Islam: acts of brutality committed against Muslims are not an excuse for Muslims to respond in kind. This idea, so clear in the traditional sources, stands in direct contrast to the positions of the fundamentalists, which through their use of Qur'ānic citations seeks to hide what ultimately can only be described as disobedience to these teachings of the Prophet.

Another Qur'ānic verse often quoted is 4:75: *And why should you not fight in the way of God and those who are weak—men, women, and children, whose cry has been: 'Our Lord, rescue us from this town, whose people are oppressors, and raise for us, from you, one who will help'*. This verse has been mentioned as justification for open warfare against the West and to inspire Muslims to fight America and her allies who threaten the Muslim lands in particular. According to our commentators, however, the reason for the revelation of 4:75 was the fact that even after the Prophet had made his migration to Medina, there were still some Muslims who remained in Makka although they could not practice their religion, and some Makkans who wished to be Muslims but would not convert out of fear of their fellow tribesmen.[91] In both cases these difficulties were due to the weakness of these people vis-à-vis the polytheistic members of their own clans who sought to oppress them with threats and even torture. Therefore, verse 4:75 was revealed to call the Muslims of Medina to a two-fold jihad:

(1) to free their brethren who were left behind in Makka from religious oppression, and

[91] Al-Ṭabarī, *Jāmi' al-bayān*, vol. 4, p. 220; Ibn Kathīr, *Tafsīr*, vol. 1, p. 698.

(2) to give those Makkans who desired to convert the ability to do so without fear of reprisals from the enemies of Islam. This clearly established context is very different from the manner in which the verse is understood by extremists, for the least that can be said is that in the West, unlike many places in the "Islamic" world itself, Muslims are basically free to worship as they see fit, nor is there any attempt to stop men or women from converting to Islam. Clearly then, the use of 4:75 as a proof text for jihad against the West and America is at best disingenuous considering the traditional understanding of the circumstances surrounding its revelation.

In addition to these verses, some cite verses 3:139 and 4:89 in their call for each Muslim to kill Americans and plunder their wealth "in any place he finds them". Verse 3:139, which says, *Do not lose heart, and do not be sad. For you will gain mastery if you are believers*, like so many misplaced quotations, actually occurs in the context of the fight against the Makkan polytheists at the battle of Uhud, while 4:89 refers to the munafiqūn or "hypocrites" among the early Islamic community. The munafiqūn, as mentioned earlier, were those Muslims who disobeyed God's commands knowingly. Many of them converted to Islam only out of a sense of the advantage that could be gained from not openly opposing the Prophet while his power was waxing. Secretly they hoped for and worked toward victory for the polytheists. It is in regard to these traitors within the Muslim community that the verse speaks with such harshness, not in reference to those outside of the umma.

One last verse that is popular in modern jihadist literature is verse 9:38:

> *O you who believe, what is the matter with you that when you are asked to go forth in the way of God, you cling heavily to the Earth. Do you prefer the life of this world to the Hereafter?* […] *Unless you go forth, He will punish you with a grievous torment and put others in your place.*

According to our commentators, this verse relates to the military expedition (*ghazwa*) led by the Prophet to Tabūk, a region in what is today northwestern Saudi Arabia. During this expedition the Muslims went out in search of Byzantine military in the region. It is said that the Muslims stayed, maneuvering in the field some ten days, but did not encounter any Byzantine forces. As regards the use of this verse, it has been quoted with the hope of encouraging Muslims today to "go forth" against America and her allies, as the early mujāhidūn did against another world power, the Byzantines. The expedition to Tabūk, however, did not constitute some kind of special case in which the Islamic limits of warfare were neglected. Although the Muslims potentially would be facing a foe far more capable and powerful than any they had yet encountered, namely, the standing army of the Byzantine Empire which had only recently conquered much of Persia, this did not constitute an excuse for transgression. Despite the danger, at no time in the expedition did the Prophet ever give orders to his army to "transgress" or discard the limits set upon jihad. Therefore, any such use of this verse within the context of encouraging such transgression is inconsistent with the historical reality of the ghazwa to Tabūk. In fact, the expedition was an occasion for establishing treaties of protection very similar to those we have mentioned in previous sections of this essay, those concluded with the people of Ayla and the Christians of Dūma.[92]

In the case of each of these verses we have cited, extremists have tried to apply them in ways which entail clear innovations from their generally accepted meanings. Such "exegesis" not only goes against basic aspects of the science of Qur'ānic commentary, it also introduces innovation into the very practice of Islam itself, by making jihad into a path of unbounded bloodshed. In this manner, the "fundamentalists" violate the fundamental principles of warfare in Islam and betray the example of the Prophet, as well as that of the first Muslims engaged in jihad. In fact their teachings are a not-so-subtle perversion of the very Islam they claim to want to preserve. So systematic is their disregard of the facts of early Islamic history and the circumstances surrounding the revelations of the Qur'ān that one is left wondering what of Islam, other than a name, would they claim to save?

CONCLUSION

We have attempted to show in this paper that, properly understood, the traditional doctrine of jihad leaves no room for militant acts like those perpetrated against the United States on 9/11. Those who carried out these crimes in the name of God and the Prophet, in fact, followed neither God nor the Prophet, but followed their own imaginings about "religion" without

[92] See Guillaume, *The Life of Muhammad*, pp. 607–608.

any serious understanding of the traditional sources of the Islamic faith. No textual justifications for their acts can be found in the Qur'ān, nor can one cite examples of such brutality and slaughter of innocents from the life of the Prophet Muhammad ﷺ or the military jihad of the early decades of Islam. The notion of a militant Islam cannot be supported by any educated reading of the source materials, be they the Qur'ān and its commentaries, the ḥadīth tradition, or the early Islamic historical works. On the contrary, what is clear when looking at these texts is the remarkable degree of acceptance and, indeed, respect that was shown to non-Muslims, Jews and Christians in particular, at a time—the early medieval period—when tolerance and acceptance of religious differences were hardly well known attitudes. Even in cases of warfare, the Muslim armies acted with remarkable dignity and principle, irrespective of the weakness or strength of their opposition. In short, the early Islamic community was characterised not by militancy, but primarily by moderation and restraint.

These traits were not in spite of the religion of Islam but because of it. This can be seen in the Qur'ān in Chapter 2, verse 143, where God says to the Muslims, *We have made you a middle people*, that is, a people who avoid extremes, and in another famous verse which says, "[...] *and He* [God] *has set the Balance* [of all things]. *Do not transgress the Balance*!" (Qur'ān 55: 7–8) Traditional Muslims saw all of life in terms of balance, from simple daily activities to fighting and jihad. Each activity had its limits and rules because God had set the balance for all things. It has primarily been certain modernized Muslims, whose influences are not the traditional teachings of the faith, but the attitudes and excesses of modernity (only cloaked with turbans and beards), who have transgressed all limits and disregarded the Balance that is true Islam.

7 | Wanton Violence in Muslimdom: Religious Imperative or Spiritual Deviation?

H.A. HELLYER

DESPITE WHAT HAS unfolded in the aftermath of events such as 9/11, 7/7 and the foiled attacks in London and at Glasgow airport in June 2007, it should be clear from the outset that "violence" is not specifically a Muslim problem. On the contrary, as Muslim propagandists never cease to point out—*ad nauseum*—historically, non-Muslim perpetrators of wanton destruction leave Muslim terrorists in the proverbial dust.

This, however, is not the point.

Historically, the erudite of the Muslim community have seldom continually blamed non-Muslims. The current mantras of "Islam is peace" and similar others have become trite in their repetition, and are a curious departure from the ways previous Muslim communities faced similar problems. Scholars of the past did not hesitate to engage in pointed self-criticism: that delicate censure that the Muslim tradition calls *muḥasaba.* This type of reflection has often been limited to the examination of deep spiritual woes and resulting traumas. Yet, muḥasaba is also a tool by which all kinds of abnormal phenomena can be examined, and expunged.

An article published in 2005 in the UK denounced the existence of "moderate Islam" as a myth, asserting that although a majority of Muslims are non-violent, they are so only by treating the Qur'ān as a "pick-and-mix selection". The article's subsequent analysis revealed a "unique" methodology; picking and mixing not only from the Qur'ān but also from the whole corpus of fourteen centuries of Muslim scholarship in a decidedly selective fashion. It is ironic then, that this is precisely the type of unqualified engagement radical *takfiris* enjoin.

The Muslim and the non-Muslim need to engage in a bit of muḥasaba in this area, for this methodology is a type that ignores the meticulous scholarship of generations of Muslim academics. Generations of academic sages have painstakingly taken the time to articulate the finer points of practise, theology and spirituality, in an unbroken chain of scholarly intellectual inheritance (the Muslim alternative to an ecclesiastical hierarchy or church), and their methodology warrants closer examination.

CLASSICAL THOUGHT: ISLAMIC INTELLECTUAL INHERITANCE ON THE DEVIATION OF MODERN RADICALS

Fortunately, the contemporary inheritors of traditional Islam disavow gratuitous violence, encourage constructive social contribution, but with the classical scholastic authority dating back to the elemental prophetic community that takfiris and others lack. For a thousand years, this is how the classical tradition developed: in a spirit of scholarly inquiry, enjoying a plurality of opinions. In so doing, they were not unmoved by emotional or personal concern, but their goal was to subordinate those concerns to the desire of honest scholastic scrutiny.

Shaykh Muhammad Afifi al-Akiti's legal opinion (fatwa) represents the considered view of a progeny of this classical tradition, as it engages with the current situation of Muslims. As a product of a thoroughly classical Muslim educational system, he does not limit himself to merely issuing an apologetic hymn, nor even a simple rebuttal of some of the poorly constructed "legal opinions" that instigated the publication of this work. Rather, he presents a scholastic refutation of not just the conclusions (which are secondary in the framework of this tradition), but the very methodology of the "pick-and-mix" style of the unqualified and the uncertified. As the author notes:

> [This is a] *fitna* (civil unrest) reeling this mercied *umma* (community), day in and day out, which is partly caused by those who, wilfully or not, misunderstand the legal discussions of the chapter on warfare outside their proper contexts which have been used by them to justify their wrong actions.

In response to this internal fitna, Shaykh Afifi thus identifies the points of Islamic law that have been misread or misinterpreted, and clarifies them with a pedagogic penetration that leaves little room for doubt for both the Muslim and the non-Muslim reader.

The text elucidates the position of Islamic law on attacking non-combatants, and confirms that any military engagement must take place through a lawfully recognised political authority—thereby negating any kind of anarchy or vigilantism. This much is hardly a surprise to any student of classical Muslim jurisprudence, but the references are useful to understand the methodology employed in reaching such a conclusion. Al-Akiti is not presenting his own "feeling", but, rather, reflecting and reporting the conclusions of the intellectual inheritance of his education. This form of Muslim education represents the refinement and evolution of a legal tradition more than a thousand years old.

One of the most useful parts of the verdict is its explanation of a most controversial issue in modern Muslim communities: the tactic of "martyrdom operations" in general and in particular in Palestine. For years, proponents of this method, regardless of the target, have employed the image of the "lone charger" as justification; al-Akiti, referring directly to the source books of Islamic law, through the matrix of a classical education, dispels any confusion. Despite the passions surrounding the issue (universally evident whenever Palestine is discussed amongst Muslims), al-Akiti approaches the issues without wilful emotion or sentiment. He firmly distinguishes between the "lone charger", who may be placing himself in jeopardy but is ultimately killed by the enemy or circumstances, and the "suicide-bomber", who takes his own life. Al-Akiti, in an unequivocal fashion, removes any legitimacy from the latter.

In so doing, he does not limit himself to the theoretical situation of targeting nameless categories of civilians, but identifies, clearly, Israeli men, women and children. Off-duty soldiers are, as al-Akiti notes, considered as "non-combatants", and thus out of bounds for attack.

He poses a poignant question, "Why was this [type of operation] not done before 1994 [the first Hamas bombing], and especially during the earlier wars, most of all during the *disasters* of 1948 and 1967?"[1]

[1] Emphasis mine. This is a reference to the end of the first Arab-Israeli war (1948) that established the state of Israel and the war of 1967 that resulted in the Israeli occupation of the West Bank, Gaza, the Golan Heights and Sinai.

Elsewhere he writes, "Yes, we are one *umma* [community], such that when one part of the macro-body is attacked somewhere, another part inevitably feels the pain". His language leaves no uncertainty regarding his obvious concern for the people of Palestine; a concern that he makes clear time and time again. One can easily see that the fatwa can also easily apply to both sides in the conflict; but in matters that he regards to be the domain of sacred law, he only permits sacred motivations of accuracy and precision. There is no pretence of piety under the guise of "defending one's own"; there is only a firm engagement with the questions in the light of law, for this is a legal affair.

Prior to this publication, no such writ of equivalent legal calibre existed in the English language, despite the urgency of this significant issue.

In his analysis of the relevant portions of classical jurisprudence in this area, al-Akiti does not limit himself to these discussions, but opens (and closes) related issues that are pertinent to contemporary Muslims: the use of bombs, commentary on the Qur'ānic verse (*ayah*) that refers to the killing of idolaters, collateral damage and the oft-cited classifications of land in Muslim jurisprudence, *dār al-ḥarb* and *dār al-Islām*.

A COMMUNITY OF PURPOSE, OR A COMMUNITY OF SCHIZOPHRENIA: MUSLIMS IN THE WEST

This last treatment leads to a discussion on an issue that may be far more pertinent to the Muslims of the West than suicide-bombing; the issue of "integration". Muslims have long been demographic minorities in non-Muslim lands, but perhaps for the first time in history Muslims are now viewed as the proverbial "fifth column"—a familiar (sic) cancer in Western societies. Empirically, this seems difficult to justify, and fine research has been undertaken by a number of authors on the connection between European societies and Islam/Muslims going back centuries.

But more damaging yet is the sentiment amongst some Muslims that they themselves do not really belong in the West; in other words, pockets of individuals in the Muslim community, often in response to the pressures they feel from the mainstream, help foster this notion of estrangement and difference themselves. The impulse to regard oneself as separate, distinct and alienated from one's neighbours, to withdraw into oneself: this is a reality for some and forms a divisive ideology of "us" against "them"; something contemporary Western societies cannot accept without challenge, whether it comes from the majority or the minority.

Identity too must be restored to its traditional and classical place, which modernity seems to have entirely misunderstood. In the wake of this bewilderment, many Muslims in the West have been left grappling with who and what they are. Considering the stresses they feel, it is not a surprise—however this mentality must now be addressed.

Beyond satisfying the questioner on the issue of denouncing violence and rejecting other negative actions, al-Akiti takes on this concept of alienation, raised in the allegation he is responding to: the role and place for Muslims in the European Union. He notes:

> [...] they [Muslims] should as a practical matter remain in these countries (of the EU), and if applicable, learn to cure the schizophrenic cultural condition in which they may find themselves—whether of torn identity in their souls or of dissociation from the general society. If they cannot do so, but find instead that their surroundings are incompatible with the life they feel they must lead, then it is recommended for them to leave and reside in a Muslim state.

There is no theoretical waffling, or inconsistency in his breakdown of the matter: Muslims should remain in these countries, but without suffering from a jumbled psychological condition.

MODERN MUSLIMS: A FAILURE OF EDUCATION AND ETIQUETTE

In the final examination of this verdict, there is the inescapable conclusion that it was written by someone who has deeply absorbed the tradition of Muslim scholarship. The point behind this verdict is not the verdict itself, but rather the fact that it is intellectually sound and juridically unassailable.

Al-Akiti emerges as a product of classical Muslim education; in this sense, he is not unique. Rather, he is a modern day continuation of the accomplished system that historically protected Muslim jurisprudence from fragmentation and divisive intellectual anarchy. It was not perfect, and it had its flaws, but it was brilliant for its time. If al-Akiti is rare today, then part of the explanation can be attributed to his own brilliance, but the more pertinent factor to take into account is the failure of modern Muslim educational systems. It is hard to ignore that the richness and depth evident in his fatwa is lacking in many of Muslimdom's madrasas. That breakdown is what produces a popular Muslim discourse that does not have many more like him.

One of the great thinkers of Islam in the twentieth century, Syed Muhammad Naquib al-Attas, identified the failures of modern Muslim communities as one deficiency: a lack of *ādāb* (manners and etiquette). In classical Muslim communities, it was understood as a matter of course that there was a certain etiquette to be observed when one approached the ritual prayer, an etiquette to be observed with other human beings, and an etiquette to be observed when drawing near to the Divine Essence.

Etiquette cannot be sacrificed on the altar of "pragmatism" or "modernity"; the greatest victory is in the upholding of the highest standards of decency and integrity, for it is against those same standards that war is being waged. With forbearance, there remains an imperative duty; to renew and restore respect for the etiquette to be observed when approaching the classical tradition of religion. Previous generations knew this, and, indeed, it is needed now more than ever. A full engagement with tradition through the appropriate etiquette focuses the intellect in a manner that al-Akiti epitomizes, and reveals that the heritage of classical Islam may be more than adequate to address the challenge of modernity. The contrary alternatives on the market at present invariably result in muddles and upheavals, the 7/7 bombings being only one chaotic manifestation.

Defending the Transgressed *by Censuring the Reckless against the Killing of Civilians*

A fatwa by Shaykh Muhammad Afifi al-Akiti

8 | Defending the Transgressed by Censuring the Reckless against the Killing of Civilians

INTRODUCTION*

GIBRIL F. HADDAD

In the Name of God, the All-Beneficent, the Most Merciful.

GENTLE READER, PEACE upon those who follow right guidance! I am honoured to present the following fatwa or "response by a qualified Muslim Scholar" against the killing of civilians by the Oxford-based Malaysian jurist of the Shāfiʿī School and my inestimable teacher, Shaykh Muhammad Afifi al-Akiti, titled *Defending the Transgressed by Censuring the Reckless against the Killing of Civilians*.

The Shaykh authored it in a few days, after I asked him to offer some guidance on the issue of targeting civilians and civilian centres by suicide bombing in response to a pseudo-fatwa by a deviant UK-based group which advocates such crimes.

Upon reading Shaykh Afifi's fatwa do not be surprised to find that you have probably never before seen such clarity of thought and expression together with breadth of knowledge of Islamic Law applied (by a non-native speaker) to define key Islamic concepts pertaining to the conduct of war and its jurisprudence, its arena and boundaries, suicide bombing, the reckless targeting of civilians and more.

* Editor's note: The following is the Introduction by Shaykh Gibril F. Haddad to the first published edition of this fatwa by Aqsa Press, United Kingdom and Warda Publications, Germany (September 2005). It is reproduced here unchanged. The text of the fatwa itself has been further revised stylistically, but the technical legal content remains exactly the same.

May it bode the best start to true education on the impeccable position of Islam squarely against terrorism in anticipation of the day all its culprits are brought to justice.

Dear Muslim reader, *as-Salāmu 'alaykum wa-raḥmatuLlāh*:

Read this luminous fatwa by Shaykh Muhammad Afifi al-Akiti carefully and learn it. Distribute it, publicise it and teach it. Perhaps we will be counted among those who do something to redress wrong, not only with our hearts as we always do, but also with our tongues, in the fashion of the inspired teachers and preachers of truth.

I have tried to strike the keynote of this fatwa in a few lines of free verse, mostly to express my thanks to our Teacher but also to seize the opportunity of such a long-expected response to remind myself of the reasons why I embraced Islam in the first place.

A *TAQRĪZ*—HUMBLE COMMENDATION

Praise to God Whose Law shines brighter than the sun!
Blessings and peace on him who leads to the abode of peace!
Truth restores honor to the Religion of goodness.
Patient endurance lifts the oppressed to the heights
While gnarling mayhem separates like with like:
The innocent victims on the one hand and, on the other,
Silver-tongued devils and wolves who try to pass for just!

My God, I thank You for a Teacher You inspired
With words of light to face down Dajjāl's advocates.
Allāh bless you, Ustādh Afifi, for ***Defending the Transgressed***
By Censuring the Reckless Against the Killing of Civilians!
Let the powers that be and every actor-speaker high and low
Heed this unique Fatwa of knowledge and responsibility.

Let every lover of truth proclaim, with pride once more,
What the war-mongers try to bury under lies and bombs:
Islam is peace and truth, the Rule of Law, justice and right!
Murderous suicide is never martyrdom but rather perversion,
Just as no flag on earth can ever justify oppression.
And may God save us from all criminals, East and West!

***

By permission of Shaykh Afifi I have done some very light editing having to do mostly with style spelling or punctuation such as standardising spacing between paragraphs, providing in-text translations of a couple of Arabic supplications, adding quotation marks to mark out textual citations and so forth.

I also provided the following alphabetical glossary of Arabic terms not already glossed by the Shaykh directly in the text.

May Allāh *Subḥānahu wa-Ta 'ālā* save Shaykh Muhammad Afifi here and hereafter, may He reward him and his teachers for this blessed work and grant us its much-needed benefits, not least of which the redress of our actions and beliefs for safety here and hereafter.

Blessings and peace on the Prophet, his Family, and all his Companions, *wal-Ḥamdu liLlāhi Rabb al-'Ālamīn*.

Gibril F. Haddad
Day of Jumu'a after Aṣr
1 Rajab al-Ḥaram 1426
5 August 2005
Brunei Darussalam

QUESTION

If you have time to address this delicate issue for the benefit of this mercied *umma* which is reeling in *fitna* day in and day out, perhaps a few blessed words might use a refutation of the following text as a springboard?

I would like you to read the following article which highlights some of the problems we are facing, and [shows] why it is quite possible that young Muslims turn to extremism. The article was issued by "*Al-Muhajiroun*" not long ago, headed by Omar Bakri Muhammad and whatever our reservations about the man, it is the content I am more concerned about, and it is possibly these types of writings which need to be confronted head-on.

Excerpt from an article by "al-Muhajiroun"

AQD UL AMAAN: THE COVENANT OF SECURITY

The Muslims living in the west are living under a covenant of security, it is not allowed for them to fight anyone with whom they have a covenant of security, abiding by the covenant of security is an important obligation upon all Muslims. However for those Muslims living abroad, they are not under any covenant with the *kuffār* in the west, so it is acceptable for them to attack the non-Muslims in the west whether in retaliation for constant bombing and murder taking place all over the Muslim world at the hands of the non-Muslims, or if it an offensive attack in order to release the Muslims from the captivity of the *kuffār*. For them, attacks such as the September 11th Hijackings is a viable option in jihad, even though for the Muslims living in America who are under covenant, it is not allowed to do operations similar to those done by the magnificent 19 on the 9/11. This article speaks about the covenant and what the scholars have said regarding Al Aqd Al Amaan - the covenant of security. [...]

Shaykh Muhammad Afifi al-Akiti's Fatwa

بسم الله الرحمن الرحيم
الحمد لله الذي يحُدُّ الحربَ ولا يُحب المعتدين والصلاة والسلام على قائد الأمة الذي هو أصبر على أذى الأعداء بفُتُوَّةٍ كاملة ومُرُوَّةٍ شاملة وعلى آله وأصحابه وجيشه أجمعين

[In the name of God, the Merciful and Compassionate. Praise be to God Who sets the boundaries of war and does not love transgressors! Blessings and peace on the General of the Community, the most patient of men in the face of the harm of enemies, with perfect chivalry and complete manliness, and upon all his Family, Companions, and Army!]

This is a collection of *masāʾil*, entitled: *Mudāfiʿ al-Maẓlūm bi-Radd al-Muhāmil ʿalā Qitāl Man Lā Yuqātil* [Defending the Transgressed by Censuring the Reckless against the Killing of Civilians], written in response to the *fitna* reeling this mercied *Umma*, day in and day out, which is partly caused by those who, willfully or not, misunderstand the legal discussions of the chapter on warfare outside its proper context (of which the technical *fiqh* terminology varies with *bāb*: *siyar*, *jihad*, or *qitāl*), which have been used by them to justify their wrong actions. May Allāh open our eyes to the true meaning [*ḥaqīqa*] of *ṣabr* and to the fact that only through it can we successfully endure the struggles we face in this *dunyā*, especially during our darkest hours; for indeed He is with those who patiently endure tribulations!

There is no *khilāf* that all the Shāfiʿī *fuqahāʾ* of today and other Sunni specialists in the Sacred Law from the Far East to the Middle East reject outright [*mardūd*] the above opinion and consider it not only an anomaly [*shādhdh*] and very weak [*wāhin*] but also completely wrong [*bāṭil*] and a misguided innovation [*bid'a ḍalāla*]: the *'amal* cannot at all be adopted by any *mukallaf.* It is regrettable too that the above was written in a legal style at which any doctor of the Law should be horrified and appalled (since it is an immature yet persuasive attempt to mask a misguided personal opinion with authority from *fiqh*, and an effort to hijack our Law by invoking one of the many *qaḍāya* of this *bāb* while recklessly neglecting others). It should serve to remind the students of *fiqh* of the importance of the forming in one's mind and being aware throughout of the *thawābit* and the *ḍawābiṭ* when reading a *furū'* text, in order to ensure that those principal rules have not been breached in any given legal case.

The above opinion is problematic in three legal particulars [*fuṣūl*]:

(1) the target [*maqtūl*]: without doubt, civilians;

(2) the authority for carrying out the killing [*āmir al-qitāl*]: as no Muslim authority has declared war, or if there has been such a declaration there is, at the time, a ceasefire [*hudna*]; and

(3) the way in which the killing is carried out [*maqtūl bih*]: since it is either *ḥarām* and is also cursed as it is suicide [*qātil nafsah*], or at the very least doubtful [*shubuhāt*] in a way such that it must be avoided by those who are religiously scrupulous [*wara'*]. Any sane Muslim who would believe otherwise and think the above to be not a crime [*jināya*] would be both reckless [*muhmil*] and deluded [*maghrūr*]. Instead, whether he realizes it or not, by doing so he would be hijacking rules from our Law which are meant for the conventional (or authorized) army of a Muslim state and addressed to those with authority over it (such as the executive leaders, the military commanders and so forth), but not to individuals who are not connected to the military or those without the political authority of the state [*dawla*].

The result in Islamic jurisprudence is: if a Muslim carries out such an attack voluntarily, he becomes a murderer and not a martyr or a hero, and he will be punished for that in the Next World.

FAṢL 1.
THE TARGET: *MAQTŪL*

The proposition: "so it is acceptable for them to attack the non-Muslims in the west", where "non-Muslims" can be taken to mean, and indeed does mean in the document, non-combatants, civilians, or in the terminology of *fiqh*: those who are not engaged in direct combat [*man lā yuqātilu*].

This opinion violates a well-known principal rule [*ḍābiṭ*] from our Law:

لا يَجوزُ قتلُ نسائِهم ولا صِبيانهم إذا لم يُقاتِلوا

> [It is not permissible to kill their (i.e., the opponents') women and children if they are not in direct combat.]

This is based on the Prophetic prohibition on soldiers from killing women and children, from the well known *ḥadīth* of Ibn 'Umar (may Allāh be pleased with them both!) related by Imāms Mālik, al-Shāfi'ī, Aḥmad, al-Bukhārī, Muslim, Ibn Mājah, Abū Dāwūd, al-Tirmidhī, al-Bayhaqī and al-Baghawī (may Allāh be well pleased with them all!) and other *ḥadīths*.

Imām al-Subkī (may Allāh be pleased with him!) made it unequivocally clear what scholars have understood from this prohibition in which the standard rule of engagement taken from it is that: "[a Muslim soldier] may not kill any women or any child-soldiers unless they are in combat directly, and they can only be killed in self-defence".[1]

It goes without saying that men and innocent bystanders who are not direct combatants are also included in this prohibition. The nature of this prohibition is so specific and well-defined that there can be no legal justification, nor can there be a legitimate *shar'ī* excuse, for circumventing this convention of war by targeting non-combatants or civilians whatsoever, and that the *ḥukm shar'ī* of killing them is not only *ḥarām* but also a Major Sin [*Kabīra*] and contravenes one of the principal commandments of our way of life.

[1] Al-Nawawī, *Majmū'*, 21:57.

FAṢL 11.
THE AUTHORITY: *ĀMIR AL-QITĀL*

The proposition: "so it is acceptable for them to attack the non-Muslims in the west whether in retaliation for constant bombing and murder taking place all over the Muslim world at the hands of the non-Muslims", where it implies that a state of war exists with a particular non-Muslim state on account of its being perceived as the aggressor.

This opinion violates the most basic rules of engagement from our Law:

أمْرُ الجهاد مَوْكولٌ إلى الإمام واجتهادِه ويلزم الرعيَّة طاعتُه فيما يراه من ذلك

> [The question of declaring war (or not) is entrusted to the executive authority and to its decision: compliance with that decision is the subject's duty with respect to what the authority has deemed appropriate in that matter.]

and:

ولإمامٍ أو أميرٍ خيارٌ بين الكفّ والقتال

> [The executive or its subordinate authority has the option of whether or not to declare war.]

Decisions of this kind for each Muslim state, such as those questions dealing with ceasefire [*'aqd al-hudna*], peace settlement [*'aqd al-amān*] and the judgment on prisoners of war [*al-ikhtār fī asīr*] can only be dealt with by the executive or political authority [*imām*] or by a subordinate authority appointed by the former authority [*amīr mansūbin min jihati l-imām*]. This is something Muslims take for granted from the authority of our *naql* [scriptures] such that none will reject it except those who betray their *'aql* [intellect]. The most basic legal reason [*'illa aṣlīyya*] is that this matter is one that involves the public interest, and thus consideration of it belongs solely to the authority:

لأنّ هذا الأمرَ من المصالح العامّة التي يختَصُّ الإمامُ بالنظر فيها

All of this is based on the well-known legal principle [*qā'ida*]:

تَصَرُّفُ الإمامِ على الرَّعِيَّة منوطٌ بالمصلحة

[The decisions of the authority on behalf of the subjects are dependent upon the public good.]

and:

فيفعل الإمامُ وجوباً الأحَظَّ للمسلمين لاجتهاده

[So the authority must act for the greatest advantage of (all of) the Muslims in making its judgement.]

Nasīḥa

Uppermost in the minds of the authority during their deliberation over whether or not to wage war should be the awareness that war is only a means and not the end. Hence, if there are other ways of achieving the aim, and the highest aim is the right to practice our religion openly (as is indeed the case in modern day Spain, for example, unlike in medieval Reconquista Spain), then it is better [*awlā*] not to go to war. This has been expressed in a few words by Imām al-Zarkashī (may Allāh be pleased with him!):

وجوبُه وجوبُ الوسائلِ لا المقاصدِ

[Its necessity is the necessity of means, not ends.]

The upshot is, whether one likes it or not, the decision and discretion and right to declare war or jihad for Muslims lie solely with the various authorities as represented today by the respective Muslim states—and not with any individual, even if he is a scholar or a soldier (and not just anyone is a soldier or a scholar)—in the same way that an authority (such as the *Qāḍī* in a court of law: *maḥkama*) is the only one with the right to excommunicate or declare someone an apostate [*murtadd*]. Otherwise, the killing would be extra-judicial and unauthorized.

Even during the period of the Ottoman caliphate, for example, another Muslim authority elsewhere, such as in the Indian subcontinent could have been engaged in a war when at the same time the Khalifa's army was at peace with the same enemy. This is how it has been throughout our long history, and this is how it will always be, and this is the reality on the ground.

FAṢL III.
THE METHOD: *MAQTUL BIH*

The proposition: "attacks such as the September 11th Hijackings is a viable option in jihad", where such attacks employ tactics—analogous to the Japanese kamikaze missions during the Second World War—that have been described variously as self-sacrificing or martyrdom or suicide missions.

There is no question among scholars, and there is no *khilāf* on this question by any *qāḍī,* mufti or *faqīh*, that this proposition and those who accept it are without doubt breaching the scholarly consensus [*mukhālifun lil-ijmāʿ*] of the Muslims since it resulted in the killing of non-combatants; moreover, the proposition is an attempt to legitimize the killing of indisputable non-combatants.

As for the kamikaze method and tactic in which it was carried out, there is a difference of opinion with some jurists as to whether or not it constitutes suicide, which is not only *ḥarām* but also cursed. In this, there are further details. (Note that in all of the following cases it is already assumed that the target is legitimate—*i.e.*, a valid military target—and that the action is carried out during a valid war when there is no ceasefire [*fī ḥāl al-ḥarb wa-lā hudnata fīh*], just as with the actual circumstance of the Japanese kamikaze attacks.)

Tafṣīl I

If the attack involves a bomb placed on the body or placed so close to the bomber that when the bomber detonates it the bomber is certain [*yaqīn*] to die, then the More Correct Position [*Qawl Aṣaḥḥ*] according to us is that it does constitute suicide. This is because the bomber, being also the *maqtūl* [the one killed], is unquestionably the same *qātil* [the immediate and active agent that kills] = *qātil nafsah* [self-killing, *i.e.*, suicide].

Furūʿ

If the attack involves a bomb (such as the lobbing of a grenade and the like), but the attacker thinks that when it is detonated, it is uncertain [*ẓann*] whether he will die in the process or survive the attack, then the Correct Position [*Qawlṣaḥīḥ*] is that this does not constitute suicide, and were he to die in this selfless act, he becomes what we properly call a martyr or hero [*shahīd*]. This is because the attacker, were he to die, is not the active, willing agent of his own death, since the *qātil* is probably someone else.

An example [*ṣūra*] of this is: when in its right place and circumstance, such as in the midst of an ongoing fierce battle against an opponent's military unit, whether ordered by his commanding officer or whether owing to his own initiative, the soldier makes a lone charge and as a result of that initiative manages to turn the tide of the day's battle but dies in the process (and not intentionally at his own hand). That soldier died as a hero (and this circumstance is precisely the context of becoming a *shahīd*—in Islamic terminology—as he died selflessly). If he survives, he wins a Medal of Honour or at the least becomes an honoured war hero and is remembered as a famous patriot (in our terminology, becoming a true *mujāhid*).

This is precisely the context of the *mas'ala* concerning the "lone charger" [*al-hājim al-waḥīd*] and the meaning of putting one's life in danger [*al-taghrīr bil-nafs*] found in all of the *fiqh* chapters concerning warfare. The *Umma*'s Doctor Angelicus, Imām al-Ghazālī (may Allāh be pleased with him!) provides the best impartial summation:

> If it is said: What is the meaning of the words of the Most High:
>
> وَلاَ تُلقُوا بِأَيْدِيكُمْ إِلَى التَّهْلُكَةِ
>
> [*and do not throw into destruction by your own hands!*]?[2]
>
> We say: There is no difference [of opinion amongst scholars] regarding the lone Muslim [soldier] who charges into the battle-lines of the [opposing] non-Muslim [army that is presently in a state of war with his army and is facing them in a battle] and fights [them] even if he knows that he will almost certainly be killed. The case might be thought to go against the requirements of the Verse, but that is not so. Indeed, Ibn 'Abbās (may Allāh be well pleased with both of them!) says: [the meaning of] "*destruction*" is not that [incident]. Instead, [its meaning] is to neglect providing

[2] Qur'ān 2:195.

[adequate] supplies [*nafaqa*: for the military campaign; and in the modern context, the state should provide the arms and equipment and so forth for that for which all of this is done] in obedience to God [as in the first part of the Verse which says: وَأَنفِقُوا فِي سَبِيلِ اللهِ (*And spend for the sake of God*)[3]].

That is, those who fail to do that will destroy themselves. [In another *ṣaḥābī* authority:] al-Barāʾa ibn ʿĀzib [al-Ansārī (may Allāh be well pleased with them both!)] says: [the meaning of] "*destruction*" is [a Muslim] committing a sin and then saying: 'my repentance will not be accepted'. [A *Tābiʿī* authority] Abū ʿUbayda says: it [the meaning of "*destruction*"] is to commit a sin and then not perform a good deed after it before he perishes. [Ponder over this!]

In the same way that it is permissible [for the Muslim soldier in the incident above] to fight the non-Muslim [army] until he is killed [in the process], that [extent and consequence] is also permissible for him [*i.e.*, the enforcer of the Law, since the *ʿāʾid* (antecedent) here goes back to the original pronoun (*ḍamīr al-aṣl*) for this *bāb*: the *muḥtasib* or enforcer, such as the police] in [matters of] law enforcement [*ḥisba*].

However, [note the following qualification (*qayd*):] were he to know [*ẓannī*] that his charge will not cause harm to the non-Muslim [army], such as the blind or the weak throwing himself into the [hostile] battle-lines, then it is prohibited [*ḥarām*], and [this latter incident] is included under the general meaning [*ʿumūm*] of "*destruction*" from the Verse [for in this case, he will be literally throwing himself into destruction].

It is only permissible for him to advance [and suffer the consequences] if he knows that he will be able to fight [effectively] until he is killed, or knows that he will be able to demoralize the hearts and minds of the non-Muslim [army]: by their witnessing his courage and by their conviction that the rest of the Muslim [army] are [also] selfless [*qilla al-mubāla*] in their loyalty to sacrifice for the sake of God [the closest modern non-Muslim parallel would be 'to die for one's country']. By this, their will to fight [*shawka*] will become demoralized [and so this may cause panic and rout them and thereby be the cause of their battle-lines to collapse].[4]

[3] Qur'ān 2:195.

[4] Al-Ghazālī, *'Iḥyā'*, 2:315–6.

It is clear that this selfless deed which any modern soldier, Muslim or non-Muslim, might perform in battle today is not suicide. It may hyperbolically be described as a 'suicidal' attack, but to endanger one's life is one thing and to commit suicide during the attack is obviously another. And as the passage shows, it is possible to have both situations: an attack that is *taghrīr bil-nafs*, which is not prohibited; and an attack that is of the *tahluka*-type, which is prohibited.

Tafṣīl II

If the attack involves ramming a vehicle into a military target and the attacker is certain to die, precisely like the historical Japanese kamikaze missions, then our jurists have disagreed over whether it does or does not constitute suicide.

Qawl A

Those who consider it a suicide argue that there is the possibility [*ẓannī*] that the *maqtūl* is the same as the *qātil* (as in *Tafṣīl* I above) and would therefore not allow for any other qualification whatsoever, since suicide is a cursed sin.

Qawl B

Whereas those who consider otherwise, even with the possibility that the *maqtūl* is the same as the *qātil*, will allow some other qualification such as the possibility that by carrying it out the battle of the day could be won. There are further details in this alternative position, such as that the commanding officer does not have the right to command anyone under him to perform this dangerous mission, so that were it to be sanctioned, it could only be when it is not under anyone else's orders and is the lone initiative of the concerned soldier (such as in defiance of the standing orders of his commanding officer).

The first of the two positions is the Preferred Position [*muttajih*] among our jurists, as the second is the rarer because of the vagueness of a precedent, and its legal details are fraught with further difficulties and ambiguities, and its opposing position [*muqābil*] carries such a weighty consequence (namely, that of suicide, for which there is *Ijmā'* that the one who commits suicide will be damned to committing it eternally forever).

In addition to this juristic preference, the first position is also preferable and better since it is the original or starting state [*aṣl*], and by invoking the well-known and accepted legal principle:

الخُروجُ مِنَ الخِلاف مُستَحَبٌ

[To avoid controversy is preferable.]

Finally, the first position is religiously safer, since owing to the ambiguity itself of the legal status of the person performing the act—whether it will result in the *maqtūl* being also the *qātil*—and since there is doubt and uncertainty over the possibility of its either being or not being the case, then this position falls under the type of doubtful matters [*shubuhāt*] of the kind [*naw'*] that should be avoided by those who are religiously scrupulous [*wara'*]. And here, the wisdom of our wise Prophet (may Allāh's blessings and peace be upon him!) is illuminated from the ḥadīth of al-Nu'mān (may Allāh be well pleased with him!):

فمَن اتَّقى الشُّبُهاتِ استَبْرَأ لِدِينِه وَعِرْضِه

[He who saves himself from doubtful matters will save his religion and his honour.][5]

Wa-Llāhu a'lam biṣ-ṣawāb! [God knows best what is right!]

Fā'ida

The original ruling [*al-aṣl*] for using a bomb (the medieval precedents: Greek fire [*qitāl bil-nār* or *ramy al-naft*] and catapults [*manjanīq*]) as a weapon is that it is *makrūh* [offensive] because it kills indiscriminately [*ya'ummu man yuqātilū wa-man lā yuqātilū*], as opposed to using rifles (medieval example: a single bow and arrow). If the indiscriminate weapon is used in a place where there are

[5] Related by Aḥmad, al-Bukhārī, Muslim, al-Tirmidhī, Ibn Mājah, al-Ṭabarānī, and al-Bayhaqī, with variants.

civilians, it becomes *ḥarām* except when used as a last resort [*min ḍarūra*] (and of course, by those military personnel authorised to do so).

ḤĀṢIL

From the consideration of the foregoing three legal particulars, it is evident that the opinion expressed regarding the *'amal* in the above article is untenable by the standards of our Sacred Law.

As to those who may still be persuaded by it and suppose that the action is something that can be excused on the pretext that there is scholarly *khilāf* on the details of *Tafṣīl* II from *Faṣl* III above (and that therefore, the *'amal* itself could at the end of the day be accommodated by invoking the guiding principle that one should be flexible with regards to legal controversies [*masā'il khilāfiyya*] and agree to disagree); know then there is no *khilāf* among scholars that that rationale does not stand, since it is well known that:

لا يُنكَرُ المُختَلفُ فيه وإنما يُنكر المجمَعُ عليه

> [The controversial cannot be denied; only (breach of) the unanimous can be denied.]

Since at the very least, it is agreed upon by all that killing non-combatants is prohibited, there is no question whatsoever that the *'amal* overall is outlawed.

The *qā'ida*, which is expressed very tersely above, means, understood correctly, that an action about which there is *khilāf* may be excused while an action that contravenes *Ijmā'* is categorically rejected.

MASĀ'IL MUFAṢṢALA

Question I

If it is said: "I have heard that Islam says the killing of civilians is allowed if they are non-Muslims."

We say: On a joking note (but ponder over this so your hearts may be opened!): the authority is not with what Islam says but with what Allāh (Exalted is He!) and His Messenger (may His blessings and peace be upon him!) have said!

But seriously: the answer is absolutely ***no***; for even a novice student of *fiqh* would be able to see that the first *ḍābiṭ* above concerns already a non-Muslim opponent in the case of a state of war having been validly declared by a Muslim authority against a particular non-Muslim enemy, even when that civilian is a subject or in the care [*dhimma*] of the hostile non-Muslim state [*Dār al-Ḥarb*]. If this is the extent of the limitation to be observed with regards to non-Muslim civilians associated with a declared enemy force, what higher standard will it be in cases if it is not a valid war or when the status of war becomes ambiguous? Keep in mind that there are more than 100 Verses in the Qur'ān commanding us at all times to be patient in the face of humiliation and to turn away from violence [*al-i'rā ḍ 'ani l-mushrikīn waṣ-ṣabr 'alā adhā al-a'dā'*], while there is only one famous Verse in which war (which does not last forever) becomes an option (in our modern context: for a particular Muslim authority and not an individual), when a particular non-Muslim force has drawn first blood.

Question II

If it is said: "What about the verse of the Qur'ān which says '*kill the unbelievers wherever you find them*' and the *ṣaḥīḥ* ḥadīth which says 'I have been ordered to fight against the people until they testify'?"

We say: It is well known among scholars that the following verse,

فَاقْتُلُوا الْمُشْرِكِينَ حَيْثُ وَجَدْتُمُوهُمْ

[*kill the idolaters wherever you find them*][6] is in reference to a historical episode: those among the Makkan Confederates who breached the Treaty of Ḥudaybiyya [*Sulḥ al- Ḥudaybiyya*] which led to the Victory of Makka [*Fatḥ Makka*], and that therefore, no legal rulings, or in other words, no practical or particular implications, can be derived from this Verse on its own. The Divine Irony and indeed Providence from the last part of the Verse, "*wherever you find them*"—which many of our *mufassir*s understood in reference to place (*i.e.*, attack them whether inside the Sacred Precinct or not)—is that the victory against the Makkans happened without a single battle taking place, whether inside the Sacred Precinct or otherwise, rather, there was a general

[6] Qur'ān 9:5.

amnesty [*wa-mannun 'alayhi bi-takhliyati sabīlihi* or *nahā 'an safki d-dimā'*] for the *Jāhilī* Arabs there. Had the Verse not been subject to a historical context, then you should know that it is of the general type [*'āmm*] and that it will therefore be subject to specification [*takhṣīṣ*] by some other indication [*dalīl*]. Its effect in lay terms, were it not related to the *Jāhilī* Arabs, is that it can only refer to a case during a valid war when there is no ceasefire.

Among the well known exegeses of "*al-mushrikīn*" from this Verse are '*an-nākithīna khāṣṣatan*' [specifically, those who have breached (the Treaty)];[7] '*al-ladhīna yuḥāribūnakum*' [those who have declared war against you];[8] and '*khāṣṣan fī mushrikī l-'arabi dūna ghayrihim*' [specifically, the *Jāhilī* Arabs and not anyone else].[9]

As for the meaning of "people" [*al-nās*] in the above well-related ḥadīth, it is confirmed by *Ijmā'* that it refers to the same "*mushrikīn*" as in the Verse of Sūra al-Tawba above, and therefore what is meant there is only the *Jāhilī* Arabs [*mushrikū l-'arab*] during the closing days of the Final Messenger and the early years of the Righteous Caliphs and not even to any other non-Muslims.

In sum, we are not in a perpetual state of war with non-Muslims. On the contrary, the original legal status [*al-aṣl*] is a state of peace, and making a decision to change this status belongs only to a Muslim authority who will in the Next World answer for their *ijtihād* and decision; and this decision is not divinely charged to any individuals—not even soldiers or scholars—and to believe otherwise would go against the well-known rule in our Law that a Muslim authority could seek help from a non-Muslim with certain conditions, including, for example, that the non-Muslim allies are of goodwill towards the Muslims:

لا يستعين بمشركين إلا بشروطٍ كأن تكونَ نيتُه حسنةً للمسلمين

Question III

If it is said: "I have heard a scholar say that 'Israeli women are not like women in our society because they are militarised'. By implication, this

[7] Al-Nawawī al-Jāwī, *Tafsīr*, 1:331.
[8] Qāḍī Ibn 'Arabī, *Aḥkām al-Qur'ān*, 2:889.
[9] Al-Jassās, *Aḥkām al-Qur'ān*, 3:81.

means that they fall into the category of women who fight and that this makes them legitimate targets but only in the case of Palestine".

We say: No properly schooled jurists from any of the Four Schools would say this as a legal judgement if they faithfully followed the juridical processes of the orthodox Schools relating to this *bāb*; for if it is true that the scholar made such a statement and meant it in the way you've implied, then not only does this violate the well-known principal rule above (*Faṣl* I: "It is not permissible to kill their women and children if they are not in direct combat"), but the supposed remarks also show a lack of sophistication in the legal particulars. If this is the case, then it has to be said here that this is not among the *masā'il khilāfiyya*, about which one can afford to agree to disagree, since it is outright wrong by the principles and the rules from our *uṣūl* and *furū'*.

Let us restate the *ḍābiṭ* again, as our jurists have succinctly summarized its rule of engagement: a soldier can only attack a female or (if applicable) child soldier (or a male civilian) in self-defence and only when *she herself* (and not someone else from her army) is engaged in direct combat. (As for male soldiers, it goes without saying that they are considered combatants as soon as they arrive on the battlefield even if they are not in direct combat—provided of course that the remaining conventions of war have been observed throughout, and that all this is during a valid war when there is no ceasefire.)

Not only is this strict rule of engagement already made clear in our secondary legal texts, but this is also obvious from the linguistic analysis of the primary proof-texts used to derive this principal rule. Hence, the form of the verb used in the scriptures, *yuqātilu*, is of the *mushāraka*-type, so that the verb denotes a direct or a personal or a reciprocal relationship between two agents: the minimum for which is one of them making an effort or attempt to act upon the other. The immediate legal implication here is that one of the two can only even be considered a legitimate target when there is a reciprocal or direct relationship.

In reality [*wāqi'*], this is not what happens on the ground (since the bombing missions are offensive in nature—they are not targeting, for example, a force that *is attacking* an immediate Muslim force; but rather the attack is directed at an overtly non-military target, so the person carrying it out can only be described as attacking it—and the target is someone unknown until only seconds before the mission reaches its termination).

In short, even if these women are soldiers, they can only be attacked when they are *in direct combat* and not otherwise. In any case, there are other overriding particulars to be considered and various conditions to be observed throughout, namely, that it must be during a valid state of war when there is no ceasefire.

Question IV

If it is said: "When a bomber blows himself up he is not directing the attack towards civilians. On the contrary, the attack is designed to target off-duty soldiers (which I was told did not mean reservists, since most Israelis are technically reservists). The innocent civilians are unfortunate collateral damage in the targeting of soldiers."

We say: There are two details here.

Tafṣīl A

Off-duty soldiers are treated as civilians.

Our jurists agree that during a valid war when there is no ceasefire, and when an attack is not aimed at a valid military target, a hostile soldier (whether male or female, whether conscripted or not) who is not on operational duty or not wearing a military uniform and when there is nothing in the soldier's outward appearance to suggest that the soldier is in combat, then the soldier is considered a non-combatant [*man lā yuqātilu*] (and in this case, must therefore be treated as a normal civilian).

A valid military target is limited to either a battlefield [*maḥall al-ma'raka* or *saḥat al-qitāl*] or a military base [*mu'askar*; medieval examples are citadel or forts; modern examples are barracks, military depots, etc.]; and certainly ***never*** can anything else such as a restaurant, a hotel, a public bus, the area around a traffic light, or any other public place be considered a valid military target, since firstly, these are not places and bases from which an attack would normally originate [*maḥall al-ra'y*]; secondly, because there is certain knowledge [*yaqīn*] that there is intermingling [*ikhtilāṭ*] with non-combatants; and thirdly, the non-combatants have not been given the option to leave the place.

As for when the soldiers are on the battlefield, the normal rules of engagement apply.

As for when the soldiers are in a barracks or the like, there is further discussion on whether the soldiers become a legitimate target, and the *Qawl Aṣaḥḥ* [the More Correct Position] according to our jurists is that they do, albeit to attack them there is *makrūh*.

Tafṣīl B

Non-combatants cannot at all be considered collateral damage except at a valid military target, for which they may be so deemed, depending on certain extenuating circumstances.

There is no *khilāf* that non-combatants or civilians cannot at all be considered collateral damage at a non-military target in a war zone, and that their deaths are not excusable by our Law, and that the one who ends up killing one of them will be sinful as in the case of murder, even though the soldier who is found guilty of it would be excused from the ordinary capital punishment [*ḥadd*], unless the killing was found to be premeditated and deliberate:

أو أتى بمعصيةٍ تُوجِب الحدَّ

If not, the murderer's punishment in this case would instead be subject to the authority's discretion [*ta'zīr*] and he would in any case be liable to pay the relevant compensation [*diya*].

As for a valid military target in a war zone, the Shāfi'ī School have historically considered the possibility of collateral damage, unlike the position held by others that it is unqualifiedly outlawed. The following are the conditions stipulated for allowing this controversial exception (in addition to meeting the most important condition of them all: that this takes place during a valid war when there is no ceasefire):

(1) The target is a valid military target.

(2) The attack is as a last resort [*min ḍarūra*] (such as when the civilians have been warned to leave the place and after a period of siege

has elapsed):

وجوبُ الإنذار قبل البَدْء بالقتْل لأنه لا يجوز أن يقتُلَ إلا مَن يُقاتل

(3) There are no Muslim civilians or prisoners.

(4) The decision to attack the target is based on a considered judgement of the executive or military leader that by doing so, there is a good chance that the battle would be won.

(Furthermore, this position is subject to *khilāf* among our jurists with regard to whether the military target can be a Jewish or Christian [*Ahl al-Kitāb*] one, since the sole primary text that is invoked to allow this exception concerns an incident restricted to the same "*mushrikīn*" as in the Verse of Sūra al-Tawba in Question II above.)

To neglect intentionally any of these strict conditions is analogous to not fulfilling the conditions [*shurūṭ*] for a prayer [*Ṣalāt*] with the outcome that it becomes invalidated [*bāṭil*] and useless [*fasād*].

This is why the means of an act [*'amal*] must be correct and validated according to the rule of Law in order for its outcome to be sound and accepted, as expressed succinctly in the following wisdom of Imām Ibn 'Aṭā Allāh (may Allāh sanctify his soul!):

مَن أشْرَقتْ بدايتُه أشرقت نهايتُه

[He who makes good his beginning will make good his ending.]

In our Law, the ends can never justify the means except when the means are in themselves permissible, or *mubāḥ* (and not *ḥarām*), as is made clear in the following famous legal principle:

وَسِيلَةُ الطَّاعَة طاعة ووسيلةُ المعصية معصية

[The means to a reward is itself a reward and the means to a sin is itself a sin.]

Hence, even a simple act such as opening a window, which on its own is only *mubāḥ* or *ḥalāl*, religiously entailing no reward nor being a sin, when a son does it with the intention of his mother's comfort on a hot summer's day before she asks for it to be opened, the originally non-consequent act itself becomes *mandūb* [recommended] and the son is rewarded in his *'amal*-account for the Next World and acquires the pleasure of Allāḥ.

WaLlāhu a'lam wa-aḥkām biṣ-ṣawāb! [God knows and judges best what is right!]

Question V

If it is said: "In a classic manual of Islamic Sacred Law I read that 'it is offensive to conduct a military expedition [*ghazw*] against hostile non-Muslims without the caliph's permission (though if there is no caliph, no permission is required).' Doesn't this entail that though it is *makrūh* for anyone else to call for or initiate such a jihad, it is permissible?"

We say:

لا غَزْوَةَ إلا في الجهاد

[There can be no battle except during a war!]

Secondary legal texts, just as with primary proof-texts (a single Verse of the Qur'ān from among the relatively few *Āyāt al-Aḥkām* or a ḥadīth from among the limited number of *Aḥadīth al-Aḥkām*), must be read and understood in context. The conclusion drawn that it is offensive or permissible for anyone other than those in authority to declare or initiate a war is evidently wrong, since it violates the principal rule of engagement discussed in *Faṣl* II above.

The context is that of endangering one's life [*taghrīr bi-nafs*] when there is already a valid war with no ceasefire, as seen in the above example from the *Iḥyā'* passage, but certainly not in executive matters of the kind of proclaiming a war and the like. This is also obvious from the terminology used: a *ghazw* [a military act, assault, foray or raid; the minimum limit in a modern example: an attack by a squad or a platoon (*katība*)] can take place only when there is a state of jihad [war], not otherwise.

Fā'ida

Imām Ibn Ḥajar (may Allāh be pleased with him!) lists the organizational structure of an army as follows: a *ba'th* [unit] and several such together, a *katība* [platoon], which is a part of a *sariyya* [company; made up of 50–100 soldiers], which is in turn a part of a *mansar* [regiment; up to 800 soldiers], which is a part of a *jaysh* [division; up to 4000 soldiers], which is a part of a *jaḥfal* [army corps; exceeding 4000 soldiers], which makes up the *jaysh 'aẓīm* [army].[10]

In our School, it is offensive but not completely prohibited for a soldier to defy, or in other words to take the initiative against the wishes of, his direct authority, whether his unit is strong or otherwise. In the modern context, this may include cases when soldier(s) disagree with a particular decision or strategy adopted by their superior officers, whether during a battle or otherwise.

The accompanying commentary to the text you quoted will help clarify this for you:

> [Original Text:] It is offensive to conduct an assault [whether the unit is strong (*man'a*) or otherwise; and some have defined a strong force as 10 men] without the permission of the authority ([Commentary:] or his subordinate, because the assault depends on the needs [of the battle and the like] and the authority is more aware about them. It is not prohibited [to go without his permission] (if) there is no grave endangering of one's life even when that is permissible in war.)[11]

Question VI

If it is said: "What is the meaning of the rule in *fiqh* that I always hear, that jihad is a *farḍ kifāya* [communal obligation] and when the *Dār al-Islām* is invaded or occupied it is a *farḍ 'ayn* [personal obligation]? How do we apply this in the context of a modern Muslim state such as Egypt?"

We say: It is *farḍ kifāya* for the eligible Muslim subjects of the state in the sense that recruitment to the military is only voluntary when the state declares war with a non-Muslim state (as for non-Muslim subjects, they evidently are not religiously obligated but can still serve). It becomes a *farḍ 'ayn* for any able-bodied Muslim when there is a conscription or

[10] Ibn Ḥajar, *Tuḥfat*, 12:4.
[11] Ibn Barakāt, *Fayḍ*, 2:309.

a nationwide draft to the military if the state is invaded by a hostile non-Muslim force, but only until the hostile force is repelled or the Muslim authority calls for a ceasefire. As for those not in the military, they have the option to defend themselves if attacked, even if they have to resort to throwing stones and using sticks:

بأيّ شيءٍ أطاقوه ولو بحجارةٍ أو عصا

Furū'

When it is not possible to prepare for war [and rally the army for war (*ijtimā' li-ḥarb*), and a surprise attack by a hostile force completely defeats the army of the state and the entire state becomes occupied] and someone [at home, for example] is faced with the choice of whether to surrender or to fight [such as when the hostile force comes knocking at the door], then he may fight. Or he may surrender, provided that he knows [with certainty] that if he resisted [arrest] he would be killed and that [his] wife would be safe from being raped [*fāḥisha*] if she were taken. If not [that is to say, even if he surrenders he knows he will be killed and his wife raped when taken], then [as a last resort] fighting [jihad] becomes personally obligatory for him.[12]

Reflect upon this legal ruling of our Religion and the emphasis placed upon preserving human life and upon the wisdom of resorting to violence only when it is *absolutely necessary* and in its proper place; and witness the conjunction between the *maqāṣid* and the *wasā'il* and the meaning of the conditions when fighting actually becomes a *farḍ 'ayn* for an individual!

Question VII

If it is said today: "In the [Shāfi'ī] *madhhab*, what are the different classifications of lands in the world? For example, *Dār al-Islām*, *Dār al-Kufr* and so forth, and what have the classical *ulema* said their attributes are?"

We say: As it is also from empirical fact [*tajriba*], Muslim scholars have classified the territories in this world into: *Dār al-Islām* [its synonyms: *Bilād al-Islām* or *Dawla Islāmiyya*; a Muslim state or territory or land or country, etc.] and *Dār al-Kufr* [a non-Muslim state, territory, etc.].

[12] Al-Bakrī, *I'ānat*, 4:197.

The definition of a Muslim state is: "any place at which a resident Muslim is capable of defending himself against hostile forces [*ḥarbiyyūn*] for a period of time is a Muslim state, where his judgements can be applied at that time and those times following it."[13] A non-Muslim who resides in a Muslim state is, in our terminology: *kāfir dhimmī* or *al-kāfir bi-dhimmatil-muslim* [a non-Muslim in the care of a Muslim state].

By definition, an area is a Muslim state as long as Muslims continue to live there and the political and executive authority is Muslim. (Think about this, for the Muslim lands are many, varied, wide and extensive; and how poor and of limited insight are those who have tried to limit the definition of what a Muslim state must be, and whether realizing it or not thus try to shrink the Muslim world!)

As for a non-Muslim state, it is the absence of a Muslim state.

As for *Dār al-Ḥarb* [sometimes called *Arḍ al-'Adw*], it is a non-Muslim state which is in a state of war with a Muslim state. Therefore, a hostile non-Muslim soldier from there is known in our books as: *kāfir ḥarbī*.

Furū'

Even if such a person enters or resides in a Muslim country that is in a state of war with his home country, provided of course he does so with the permission of the Muslim authority (such as entering with a valid visa and the like), the sanctity of a *kāfir ḥarbī*'s life is protected by Law, just like the rest of the Muslim and non-Muslim subjects of the state.[14] In this case, his legal status becomes a *kāfir ḥarbī bi-dhimmati l-imām* [a hostile non-Muslim under the protection of the Muslim authority], and for all intents and purposes he becomes exactly like the non-Muslim subjects of the state. In this way, the apparent difference between a *dhimmī* and a *ḥarbī* non-Muslim becomes only an academic exercise and a distinction in name only.

The implications of this rule for the pious, God-fearing and Law-abiding Muslims are not only that to attack non-Muslims becomes something illegal and an act of disobedience [*ma'ṣiya*], but also that the steps taken by the Muslim authority and enforcers, such as in Malaysia

[13] Ba'alawī, *Bughyat*, 254.

[14] Al-Kurdī, *Fatāwā*, 211–2.

or Indonesia today, to protect their places, including churches or temples, from the threat of killings and bombings, are included under the *bāb* of *amr bi-ma'rūf wa nahy 'ani l-munkar* [the duty to intervene when another is acting wrongly; in the modern context: enforcing the Law], even if the Muslim enforcers [*muḥtasib*] die in the course of protecting non-Muslims.

Question VIII

If it is said: "What land classification are we in the European Union, and what is the *ḥukm* of those who are here? Should they theoretically leave?"

We say: It is clear that the countries in the Union are non-Muslim states, except for Turkey or Bosnia, for example, if they are a part of the Union. The status of the Muslims who reside and are born in non-Muslim states is the reverse of the above non-Muslim status in a Muslim state: *al-muslim bi-dhimmati l-kāfir* [a Muslim in the care of a non-Muslim state] and from our own Muslim and religious perspective, whether we like it or not, there are similarities to the status of a guest which should not be forgotten.

There is precedent for this status in our Law. The answer to your question is that they should as a practical matter remain in these countries, and if applicable, learn to cure the schizophrenic cultural condition in which they may find themselves—whether of torn identity in their souls or of dissociation from the general society. If they cannot do so, but find instead that their surroundings are incompatible with the life they feel they must lead, then it is recommended for them to leave and reside in a Muslim state. This status is made clear in the fatwa of the *Muḥaqqiq*, Imām al-Kurdī (may Allāh be pleased with him!):

> He (may the mercy of Allāh—Exalted is He!—be upon him!) was asked: In a territory ruled by non-Muslims, they have left the Muslims [in peace] other than that they pay tax [*māl*] every year just like the *jizya*-tax in reverse, for when the Muslims pay them, their protection is ensured and the non-Muslims do not oppose them [*i.e.*, do not interfere with them]. Thereupon, Islam becomes practiced openly and our Law is established [meaning that they have the freedom to practice their religious duty in the open and in effect become

> practicing Muslims in that non-Muslim society]. If the Muslims do not pay them, the non-Muslims could massacre them by killing or pillage. Is it permissible to pay them the tax [and thereby become residents there]? If you say it is permissible, what is the ruling about the non-Muslims mentioned above when they are at war [with a Muslim state]: would it or would it not be permissible to oppose them and if possible, take their money? Please give us your opinion!

The answer:

> Insofar as it is possible for Muslims to practice their religion openly with what they can have power over, and they are not afraid of any threat [*fitna*] to their religion if they pay tax to the non-Muslims, it is permissible for them to reside there. It is also permissible to pay them the tax as a requirement of it [residence]; rather, it is obligatory [*wājib*] to pay them the tax for fear of their causing harm to the Muslims. The ruling about the non-Muslims at war as mentioned above, because they protect the Muslims [in their territory], is that it would not be permissible for the Muslims to murder them or to steal from them.[15]

The *ḍābiṭ* for this *mas'ala* is:

وإنْ قَدَرَ على إظهار الدين ولم يخَفِ الفتنة في دينه ونفسه وماله لم تجِبْ عليه الهجرةُ

> [If someone is able to practice his religion openly and is not afraid of threat to his religion, life and property, then emigration is not obligatory for him.]

Furūʿ

Our Shāfiʿī jurists have discussed details concerning the case of Muslims residing in a non-Muslim state, and they have divided the legal rulings about their emigration from it to a Muslim state into four sorts (assuming that an individual is capable and has the means to emigrate):

1. *Ḥarām*: it is prohibited for them to leave when they are able to defend their territory from a hostile non-Muslim force or withdraw from it (as in

[15] Al-Kurdī, *Fatāwā*, 208.

the case of a border state, buffer area or disputed territory) and do not need to ask for help from a Muslim state. The reason is that their place of residence is already, technically [*ḥukman*], a 'Muslim state' even though not in name [*ṣūratan*], since they are able to practice their religion openly even though the political or executive authority is not Muslim; and if they emigrated it would cease to be so. This falls under the *fiqhī* classification of *Dār Kāfir Ṣūratan Lā Ḥukman*, which is equivalent to *Dār Islām Ḥukman Lā Ṣūratan*.

2. *Makrūh*: it is offensive to leave their place of residence when it is possible for them to practice their religion openly, and they wish to do so openly.

3. *Mandūb*: leaving becomes recommended only when it is possible for them to practice their religion openly, but they do not wish to do so.

4. *Wājib*: it becomes obligatory to leave when it is the only remaining option, that is, when practicing their religion openly is not possible. A legal precedent is the case after the Reconquista in Spain (which is no longer the case today) when the Five Pillars of the Faith were actively proscribed, so that, for example, the Muslim houses were required to keep their doors open after sunset during the fasting month of Ramaḍān in order that the authority could see that there was no breaking of the fast.

Question IX

If it is said: "Would you say that in the modern age with all the considerations surrounding sovereignty and inter-connectedness, these classical labels do not apply any longer, or do we have sufficient resources in the School to continue using these same labels?"

We say: As Imām al-Ghazālī used to say:

إذا عُرِفَ المعنى فلا مُشَاحَّةَ في الأسامي

[Once the real meaning is understood, there is no need to quibble over names.]

Labels can never be relied upon; it is the meaning behind them that must be properly understood. Once they are unpacked, they immediately become relevant for all times; just as with the following loaded terms: jihad, *mujāhid* and *shahīd*. The result for Muslims who fail to notice the relevance and fail to connect the dots of our own inherited medieval terms with the modern world may be that they will live in a schizophrenic cultural reality and will be unable to associate themselves with the surrounding society and will not be at peace [*sukūn*] with the rest of creation. Just as the *sabab al-wujūd* of this article is a Muslim's misunderstanding of his own medieval terminology from a long and rich legacy, the *fitna* in the world today has been the result of those who misunderstand our Law.

Pay heed to the words of Mawlānā Rūmī (may Allāh sanctify his secrets!):

> *Go beyond names and look at the qualities, so that they may show you the way to the essence.*
>
> *The disagreement of people takes place because of names. Peace occurs when they go to the real meaning.*
>
> *Every war and every conflict between human beings has happened because of some disagreement about names.*
>
> *It's such an unnecessary foolishness, because just beyond the arguing there's a long table of companionship, set and waiting for us to sit down.*

End of the *masā'il* section.

TATIMMA

It is truly sad that despite our sophisticated and elaborate set of rules of engagement and in spite of the strict codes of warfare and the chivalrous disciplines which our soldiers are expected to observe, all having been thoroughly worked out and codified by the orthodox jurists of the *Umma* from among the generations of the *Salaf*, there are today in our midst those who are not ashamed to depart from these sacred conventions in favour of opinions espoused by persons who are not even trained in the Sacred Law at all let alone enough to be a *qāḍī* or a *faqīh*—the rightful heir and source from which they should receive practical guidance in the first place. Instead they rely on engineers or scientists and on those who are not among its *ahl*, yet speak in the name of our Law. With these "reformist" preachers and *dā'ī*'s comes a departure from the traditional ideas about the rules of *siyar*/jihad/*qitāl*, *i.e.*, warfare. Do they not realize that by doing so and by following them they will be ignoring the limitations and restrictions cherished and protected by our pious forefathers and that they will be turning their backs on the *Jamā'a* and *Ijmā'* and that they will be engaging in an act for which there is no accepted legal precedent within orthodoxy in our entire history? Have they forgotten that part of the original *maqṣad* of warfare/jihad was to limit warfare itself and that warfare for Muslims is not total war, so that women, children and innocent bystanders are not to be killed and property not to be needlessly destroyed?

To put it plainly, there is simply no legal precedent in the history of Sunni Islam for the tactic of attacking civilians and overtly non-military targets. Yet the awful reality today is that a minority of Sunni Muslims, whether in Iraq or Beslan or elsewhere, have perpetrated such acts in the name of jihad and on behalf of the *Umma*. Perhaps the first such mission to break this long and admirable precedent was the Hamas bombing on a public bus in Jerusalem in 1994—not that long ago. (Reflect on this!)

Immediately after the incident, the almost unanimous response of the orthodox Shāfi'ī jurists from the Far East and the Hadramawt was not only to make clear that the minimum legal position from our Sacred Law is untenable for persons who carry out such acts, but also to warn the *Umma* that by going down that path we would be compromising the optimum way of *Iḥsān* and that we would thereby be running a real risk of losing the moral and religious high ground. Those who still defend this tactic, invoking blindly a nebulous *uṣūlī* principle that it is justifiable out of *ḍarūra* while ignoring the *far'ī* strictures, must look long and hard at what they are doing and ask the question: was it ***absolutely necessary***, and if so, why was this not done before 1994, and especially during the earlier wars, most of all during the disasters of 1948 and 1967?

How could such a tactic be condoned by one of our Rightly Guided Caliphs and a heroic fighter such as 'Alī (may Allāh ennoble his face!), who when in the Battle of the Trench his notorious non-Muslim opponent, who was seconds away from being killed by him, spat on his noble face, immediately left him alone. When asked later his reasons for withdrawing when Allāh clearly gave him power over him, he answered: "I was fighting for the sake of God, and when he spat in my face I feared that if I killed him it would have been out of revenge and spite!" Far from being an act of cowardice, this characterizes Muslim chivalry: fighting, yet not out of anger.

In actual fact, the only precedent for this tactic from Muslim history is the cowardly terrorism carried out by the "Assassins" of the Nizārī Ismā'īlīs. Their most famous victim from a suicide mission was the wise minister and the Defender of the Faith who could have been alive to deal with the *fitna* of the Crusades: Niẓām al-Mulk, the Jamāl al-Shuhadā' (may Allāh encompass him with His mercy!), assasinated on Thursday, the 10th of the holy month of Ramaḍān 485, or October 14th, 1092.

Ironically, in the case of Palestine, the precedent was set not by Muslims but by early Zionist terrorist gangs such as the Irgun, who, for example, infamously bombed the King David Hotel in Jerusalem on 22nd July 1946. So ask yourself as an upright and God-fearing believer, whose every organ will be interrogated: do you really want to follow the footsteps and the models of those Zionists and the heterodox Isma'īlīs, instead of the path taken by our Beloved (may Allāh's blessings and peace be upon him!), who for almost half of the (twenty-three) years of his mission endured Makkan persecution, humiliation and insults? Is anger your only strength? If so, remember the Prophetic advice that it is from the Devil. And is *ḍarūra* your only excuse for following them instead into their condemned lizard-holes? Do you think that any of our famous *mujāhids* from history, such as 'Alī, Ṣalāḥ al-Dīn, and Muḥammad al-Fātiḥ (may Allāh be well pleased with them all!) will ever condone the article you quoted and these acts today in Baghdad, Jerusalem, Cairo, Bali, Casablanca, Beslan, Madrid, London and New York, some of them committed on days when it is traditionally forbidden by our Law to fight: Dhū l-Qa'da and al- Ḥijja, Muḥarram and Rajab? Every person of *fiṭra* will see that this is nothing other than a sunna of perversion.

This is what happens to the Banū Adam when the *wahm* is abandoned by *'aql*, when one of the *maqāṣid* justifies any *wasīla*, when the realities of *furū'* are indiscriminately overruled by generalities of *uṣūl*, and most tragically, as illustrated from the eternal blunder of Iblīs, when Divine *tawakkul* is replaced by basic *nafs*.

Yes, we are one *Umma* such that when one part of the macro-body is attacked somewhere, another part inevitably feels the pain. Yet at the same time, our own history has shown that we have also been a wise and sensible, instead of a reactive and impulsive, *Umma*. That is the secret of our success, and that is where our strengths will always lie as has been promised by Divine Writ: in *ṣabr* and in *tawakkul*. It is already common knowledge that when Jerusalem fell to the Crusading forces on the 15th of July 1099 and was occupied by them, and despite its civilians having been raped, killed, tortured and plundered and the *Umma* at the time humiliated and insulted—acts far worse than what can be imagined in today's occupation—that it took more than 100 years of patience and legitimate struggle under the Eye of the Almighty before He allowed Ṣalāḥ al-Dīn to liberate Jerusalem. We should have been taught from childhood by our fathers and mothers about the need to prioritize and about how to reconcile the spheres of our global concerns with those of our local responsibilities—as we will definitely not escape the questioning in the grave about the latter—so that by this insight we may hope that our response will not be disproportionate nor inappropriate. This is the true meaning [*ḥaqīqa*] of the true advice [*naṣīḥa*] of our Beloved Prophet (may Allāh's blessings and peace be upon him!): to leave what does not concern one [*tark ma lā ya'nīh*], where one's time and energy could be better spent in improving the lot of the Muslims today or benefiting others in this world.

Yes, we will naturally feel the pain when any of our brothers and sisters die unjustly anywhere when their deaths have been caused directly by non-Muslims, but it ***must*** be the more painful for us when they die in Iraq, for example, when their deaths are caused directly by the self-destroying/martyrdom/suicide missions carried out by one of our own. On *tafakkur*, the second pain should make us realize that missions of this sort, when the means and the legal particulars are all wrong—by scripture and reason—are not only a scourge for our non-Muslim neighbours but a plague and great *fitna* for this mercied *Umma*, and desire *inṣāf* so that out of *maṣlaḥa* and the general good, it must be stopped.

To this end, we could sum up a point of law tersely in the following maxim:

لا يَجْعَلُ الظُّلمَانِ الثَّانِيَ حقًّا

[Two wrongs do not make a right.]

If the first pain becomes one of the mitigating factors and ends up being used as a justification by our misguided young to retaliate in a manner which our Sacred Law definitely and without doubt outlaws (which makes your original article the more appalling, as its author will have passed the special age of 40), then the latter pain should by its graver significance generate a greater and more meaningful response. With this intention, we may hope that we shall regain our former high ground and reputation and rediscover our honour and chivalrous qualities and be no less brave.

I end with the first ever Verse revealed in the Qur'ān which bestowed the military option only upon those in a position of authority:

وقَاتِلُوا فِي سَبِيلِ اللهِ الَّذِينَ يُقَاتِلُونَكُمْ وَلاَ تَعْتَدُوا إِنَّ اللهَ لاَ يُحِبُّ الْمُعْتَدِينَ

[*And fight for the sake of God those who fight you: but do not commit excesses, for God does not love those who exceed (i.e., the Law).*][16]

Even then, peace is preferred over war:

وَإِنْ جَنَحُوا لِلسَّلْمِ فَاجْنَحْ لَهَا وَتَوَكَّلْ عَلَى اللهِ

[*Now if they incline toward peace, then incline to it, and place your trust in God.*][17]

Even if you think that the authority in question has decided wrongly and you disagree with their decision not to war with the non-Muslim state upon which you wish war to be declared, then take heed of the following Divine command:

يَا أَيُّهَا الَّذِينَ ءَامَنُوا أَطِيعُوا اللهَ وأَطِيعُوا الرَّسُولَ وَأُولِى الأَمْرِ مِنْكُمْ

[*O believers, obey Allāh, and obey the Messenger, and those with authority among you!*][18]

If you still insist that your authority should declare war with the non-Muslim state upon which you wish war to be declared, then the most you could do in this capacity is to lobby your authority for it. However, if your anger is so unrestrained that its fire brings out the worst in you to the

[16] Qur'ān 2:190.
[17] Qur'ān 8:61.
[18] Qur'ān 4:59.

point that your disagreement with your Muslim authority leads you to declare war on those you want your authority to declare war on, and you end up resorting to violence, then know with certainty that you have violated our own religious Laws. For then you will have taken the *Sharī'a* into your own hands. If indeed you reach the point of committing a violent act, then know that by our own Law you would have been automatically classified as a rebel [*ahl al-baghy*] whom the authority has the right to punish: even if the authority is perceived to be or is indeed corrupt [*fāsiq*]. (The definition of rebels is: "Muslims who have disagreed [not by heart or by tongue but by hand] with the authority even if it is unjust [*jā'ir*] and they are correct [*'adilūn*]".)[19]

That is why, my brethren, when the military option is not a legal one for the individuals concerned, you must not lose hope in Allāh; and let us be reminded of the words of our Beloved (may Allāh's blessings and peace be upon him!):

أفضَلُ الجِهَادِ كَلِمَةُ حَقٍّ عِنْدَ سُلطَانٍ جَائِرٍ

[The best jihad is a true (*i.e.*, brave) word in the face of a tyrannical ruler.][20]

For it is possible still, and especially today, to fight injustice or *ẓulm* or *ṭāghūt* in this *dunyā* through your tongue and your words and through the pen and the courts, which still amounts in the Prophetic idiom to jihad, even if not through war. As in the reminder [*tadhkira*] of the great scholar, Imām al-Zarkashī: war is only a means to an end and as long as some other way is open to us, that other way should be the course trod upon by Muslims.

Ma shā' Allāh, how true indeed are the Beloved's words, so that the latter *mujāhid* or activist will be no less brave or lacking in any courage with his or her campaign for a just cause in an oppressive country or one needing reforms than the former *mujāhid* or patriot who fought bravely for his country in a just war.

[19] Al-Nawawī, *Majmū'*, 20:337.

[20] From a ḥadīth of Abū Sa'īd al-Khudrī (may Allah be well pleased with him!) among others, which is related by Ibn al-Ja'd, A ḥmad, Ibn Ḥumayd, Ibn Mājāh, Abū Dāwūd, al-Tirmidhī, al-Nasā'ī, Abū Ya'lā, Abū Bakr al-Rūyānī, al-Ṭabarānī, al- Ḥākim, and al-Bayhaqī, with variants.

فاتَّقِ اللهَ ورَاجِعْ مُفَاتَّشَةَ نَفسِك وإصلاحَ فسادِها وهو حسبنا ونعم الوكيل ولا حول ولا قُوَّةَ إلا بالله
العلِيِّ العظيم وصلواتُه على سيدنا محمدٍ وآله وسلَّمْ ورضي اللهُ تبارك وتعالى عن ساداتنا أصحابِ
رسول الله أجمعين وعنَّا معهم وفيهم ويجْعَلَنا من حِزْبِهم برحمتك يا أرحمَ الرَّاحمين آمين

[Fear God, and go back to controlling your self and to curing your wickedness! For indeed, He is enough for us: what an excellent guardian! There is no help nor power except through God, the High and Mighty! May His blessings and peace be upon our master, Muḥammad, and his Family! And may He be pleased with our leaders, the Companions of the Messenger of God, one and all! And may we be together with them and in their company, and may He make us among their Troop. By Your Mercy, O Most Merciful of those who show mercy, Amen!]

May this be of benefit.

With heartfelt wishes for *salām* and *ṭayyiba*
from Oxford to Brunei,
Muhammad Afifi al-Akiti
16th Jumādā' II 1426
23rd July 2005

SELECT BIBLIOGRAPHY

Ba'alawī, 'Abd al-Raḥmān. *Bughyat al-Mustarshidīn fī Talkhīṣ Fatāwā ba'ḍ al-Muta'akhkhirīn.* Bulaq, 1309 H.

al-Bakrī. *Ḥāshiyat I'ānat al-Ṭālibīn.* 4 vols. Bulaq, 1300 H.

al-Ghazālī. *Iḥyā' 'Ulūm al-Dīn.* Edited by Badawī Aḥmad Ṭabānaḥ 4 vols. Cairo: Dār Iḥyā' al-Kutub al-'Arabiyya, 1957.

Ibn 'Arabī, Qāḍī. *Aḥkām al-Qur'ān.* Edited by 'Alī Muḥammad al-Bajawī. 4 vols. Cairo: Dār Iḥyā' al-Kutub al-'Arabiyya, 1957–8.

Ibn Barakāt. *Fayḍ al-Ilāh al-Mālik fī Ḥall Alfāẓ 'Umdat al-Sālik wa-'Uddat al-Nāsik.* Edited by Muṣṭafā Muḥammad Imāra. 2 vols. Singapore: al- Ḥaramayn, 1371 H.

Ibn Ḥajar al-Haytamī. *Tuḥfat al-Muḥtāj bi-Sharḥ al-Minhāj al-Nawawī* in *Ḥawāshī al-Shirwānī wa-Ibn Qāsim 'alā Tuḥfat al-Muḥtāj.* Edited by Muḥammad 'Abd al-'Azīz al-Khālidī. 13 vols. Beirut: Dār al-Kutub al-Ilmiyya, 1996.

al-Jassās, *Aḥkām al-Qur'ān.* 3 vols. Istanbul: Dār al-Khilāfa al-'Āliya, 1335–1338.

al-Kurdī. *Fatāwā al-Kurdī al-Madanī.* In *Qurrat al-'Ayn bi-Fatāwā 'Ulamā' al-Ḥaramayn.* Edited by Muḥammad 'Alī ibn Ḥusayn al-Mālikī. Bogor: Maktabat 'Arafāt, n.d.

al-Nawawī. *al-Majmū' Sharḥ al-Muhadhdhab.* Edited by Maḥmūd Maṭrajī. 22 vols. Beirut: Dār al-Fikr, 1996.

al-Nawawī al-Jāwī. *Marāḥ Labīd Tafsīr al-Nawawī: al-Tafsīr al-Munīr li-Ma'ālim al-Tanzīl al-Mufassir 'an Wujūh Maḥāsin al-Ta'wīl al-Musammā Marāḥ Labīd li-Kashf Ma'nā Qur'ān Majīd.* 2 vols. Bulaq, 1305 H.

GLOSSARY OF TERMS

ﷺ = An invocation of God's blessings and peace for the Prophet Muhammad: "Peace and blessings of God be upon him."

عليه السلام = An invocation of God's peace upon a prophet: "Peace be upon him."

ahl = [1] people; [2] qualified adherents or practitioners

'aql = intellect, reason

Aḥādīth al-Aḥkām = ḥadīthic proof-texts for legal rulings

'amal = deed, action

aṣl = see *uṣūl*

Āyāt al-Aḥkām = Qur'ānic proof-texts for legal rulings

bāb = chapter or legal subject

Banū Ādam = human beings

ḍābiṭ = see *ḍawābiṭ*

ḍarūra = necessity

ḍawābiṭ = pl. of *ḍābiṭ* = standard or principal rule

Doctor Angelicus = Angelic Scholar, a title given to Thomas Aquinas, the great theologian of the Western Church

dā'ī = summoner or preacher

dunyā = this world, "this life"

fā'ida = benefit

faqīh = see *fiqh*

farḍ 'ayn = personal obligation

farḍ kifāya = communal obligation

far'ī = adj. from *far'*, see *furū'*

faṣl = see *fuṣūl*

fatwa = legal opinion, legal response

fiqh = Islamic jurisprudence, the expertise of the *faqīh*; adj, *fiqhī* = legal

fitna = strife, temptation, seduction, delusion, chaos, trial and tribulation

fiṭra = sane mind and soul, primordial disposition

fuqahā' = pl. of *faqīh* (q.v.)

furū' = pl. of *far'*, [1] branches (of the Law), secondary legal texts; [2] corollaries

fuṣūl = pl. of *faṣl* = sections or legal particulars

ḥadīth = a saying of the Prophet Muhammad ﷺ

ḥalāl = lawful, permitted

ḥarām = categorically prohibited, unlawful

ḥāṣil = legal outcome

ḥukm [*shar'ī*] = legal status, legal ruling

Iblīs = Satan

Iḥsān = Excellence, the pinnacle of religious practice

ijmā' = Consensus

ijtihād = independent judgement, personal decision

inṣāf = fairness, setting things right

Jāhilī = lit., ignorant; a pre-Islamic or pagan Arab

Jamā'a = the Orthodox Community

Jamāl al-Shuhadā' = The Beauty of Martyrs, the title of the murdered vizier Niẓām al-Mulk

Jihad = moral or military struggle by the *mujāhid*

khilāf = (juridical) disagreement

khilāfiyya = fem. adjective from *khilāf* = having to do with (juridical) disagreement

madhhab = school of Law

makrūh = detestable, abhorrent, abominable, disliked, legally offensive

maqāṣid = pl. of *maqṣad,* objective or ends

maqṣad = see *maqāṣid*

masā'il = pl. of *mas'ala* = question or legal discussion or case

masā'il mufaṣṣala = detailed questions and answers

mas'ala = see *masā'il*

maṣlaḥa = welfare, public/general good

mubāḥ = indifferently permissible

mufassir = exegete

mufti = one who formulates fatwas or formal legal responses

Muḥaqqiq = The Careful Examiner, a title given to Imām al-Kurdī, one of the last great jurists of the Shafi'ī School

mujāhid = one who does jihad (*q.v.*)

mukallaf = legally-responsible Muslim

mushāraka = mutual or reciprocal matter

nafs = ego, self

nasīḥa = faithful, sincere advice

qaḍāyā = pl. of *qadiyya* = issue or legal context

qāḍī = judge in an Islamic court of law

qā'ida = see *qawā'id*

qātil nafsah = self-killer, suicide

qawā'id = pl. of *qā'ida* = maxim or legal principle

qawl = saying or legal position

qitāl = warfare, battle

sabab al-wujūd = raison d'etre

ṣabr = patient endurance and fortitude

Ṣaḥābī = Companion of the Prophet Muḥammad, upon whom blessings and peace

Salaf = Pious Predecessors, early authorities

shahīd, pl. *shuhadā'* = self-sacrificing believer who dies for the sake of God alone, "martyr"

shar'ī = adj. legitimate in the eyes of the *Sharī'a* (Islamic Law), lawful, legal

siyar = military expeditions

sunna = way, path

sūra = a chapter of the Qur'ān

Tābi'ī = Successor of the Companions

tafakkur = reflection

tafṣīl = detailed legal discussion

tahluka = self-destruction

taghrīr bil-nafs = risking one's life

tatimma = conclusion

tawakkul = reliance upon God

thawābit = pl. of *thābit* = axiom

Umma = the Muslim Community

uṣūl = pl. of *aṣl* = foundational principle; adj. *uṣūlī*

wahm = imaginative faculty or emotions

wasā'il = pl. of *wasīla,* means

wasīla = see *wasā'il*